About the Author

Stephen D'Arcy is an associate professor in the Department of Philosophy at Huron University College, at Western University, in London, Ontario. He teaches courses in moral and political philosophy, and publishes in the areas of democratic theory and practical ethics. He is a long-time social activist and protest organizer.

More Praise for Languages of the Unheard

"Through exploring the concept of militancy from all angles and depths, D'Arcy shows that the more society tries to stifle even the discussion of militancy, the more loudly and forcefully those without a voice will be compelled to speak. In the end, D'Arcy resolves this paradox by pointing out that the voice of militancy will only be silenced when we create a true democracy where everyone has a voice." (Ann Hansen, author of *Direct Action: Memoirs of an Urban Guerrilla*)

"Contrary to those liberals and social democrats who argue that militant activism is antidemocratic, Stephen D'Arcy makes a sustained argument coming from within democratic theory that forms of militant disruptive protest can instead be seen as crucial to defending and expanding participatory forms of democracy." (Gary Kinsman, author of *The Regulation of Desire*)

"I highly recommend this book to all people, young and old, and especially to Indigenous youth who are at the forefront of this generation of activists. It is important to know when and where protests, blockades, or militant actions have been successful. And why!" (Jeannette Corbiere Lavell, founding and honourary board member, Ontario Native Women's Association)

Languages of the Unheard

Why Militant Protest is Good for Democracy

Stephen D'Arcy

LONDON | NEW YORK

Languages of the Unheard was published in 2014 by Zed Books Ltd,
7 Cynthia Street, London N1 9JF, UK and Room 400, 175 Fifth Avenue,
New York, NY 10010, USA

www.zedbooks.co.uk

First published in Canada in 2013 by Between the Lines, Toronto, Canada

www.btlbooks.com

Typeset in Utopia by Steve Izma
Index: Martin Boyne
Cover designed by roguefour.co.uk
Printed and bound by CPI Group (UK) Ltd, Croydon, CR0 4YY

Distributed in the USA exclusively by Palgrave Macmillan, a division of
St Martin's Press, LLC, 175 Fifth Avenue, New York, NY 10010, USA

A catalogue record for this book is available from the British Library

Library of Congress Cataloging in Publication Data available

ISBN 978 1 78360 163 9 hb
ISBN 978 1 78360 162 2 pb

For my parents

Contents

Introduction: Militancy as a Civic Virtue

"WHAT WE MUST SEE," Martin Luther King once insisted, "is that a riot is the language of the unheard."[1] Recourse to rioting, he suggested, is seldom a marker of irrationality or mob psychology. More often, it is an attempt by marginalized people to find their voice, to gain a hearing, to assert their refusal to be silenced or ignored.

King's remark was as controversial as it was illuminating, yet he stopped short of depicting riots as defensible. He insisted only that they were understandable – a frustrated response to persistent injustice that made some sense in the face of long experience with intransigent elites and unresponsive systems of power. But his wording hints at the possibility of a stronger view: that these outbursts of rebellion might sometimes be defensible, even admirable, because they make it impossible to ignore the grievances of the exploited and the oppressed.

What if we, today, were to adopt this interpretation of riots? How might this idea transform our understanding and evaluation of these spontaneous revolts? And could this understanding be extended to other forms of confrontational protest and rebellion: to general strikes, sit-ins, road blockades and occupations, to the monkeywrenching saboteur, the black bloc street fighter, or even the armed insurgent? Could these forms of militancy be regarded, in the same way, as languages of the unheard?

In pursuing these questions, there can be no better guide than King himself, whose writings and speeches are peppered with enthusiastic references to what he called "the marvellous new militancy" of the 1960s.[2] This book borrows freely from the terminology that he uses when discussing confrontational protest. Key themes, especially in the opening chapters, emerge directly from engagement with his work: an account of the militant's vocation as giving a voice to the voiceless; a definition of militancy as grievance-motivated, adversarial, and confrontational collective action; a typology of defiance, disruption, destruction, and armed force as four distinct styles of militancy; and finally, an insistence on the importance of distinguishing – although I diverge from his way of distinguishing – sound from unsound militancy.

But not everyone will join me in endorsing King's judgment that "militant organization" is "indispensible . . . to our struggle"[3] for democracy and social justice. Indeed, militancy has many critics. Some are relatively easy to dismiss, for instance, the grim, law-and-order crackdown advocates, well described by King himself as being "more devoted to 'order' than to justice."[4] Their weak attachment to the importance of social justice and public autonomy is reason enough for them to wring their hands when they see bold action against racism or poverty, colonialism or sexism. Other critics of militancy, however, are sincerely committed to the resolution of urgent grievances. Their concerns about using confrontational means to this end, therefore, cry out for a serious response. These are the many social justice advocates whose liberal attachments to notions of equality and democracy are genuine, and whose numbers swell the ranks of many popular demonstrations and social movement organizations.

Their concern – which I call the liberal objection – is that by resorting to forceful pressure, rather than consensus-building and reason-guided public discussion, the militant protester in effect reverts to force, rather than dialogue, and in this way breaks with the democratic ideal. Can militants offer a principled reply, or do they have to follow those advocates of militancy (notably, anarchist writer Peter Gelderloos[5]) who disavow the claim to be on the side of democracy, thus seemingly conceding the liberal's main point?

I believe that a principled and convincing rebuttal to the liberal objection is available to militant protesters. And this is what I offer in this book: a normative standard, by appeal to which it can be shown when and on what basis militancy is a support, not a danger, to democratic norms.

In the response that I propose, I break with King in one crucial respect. Unlike King, I am unconvinced by one of the most popular standards of legitimacy for militant resistance, namely, the fixation on the difference between "violence" and "nonviolence." Time and again, one hears that protesters went too far by resorting to violence, or that the people who indulge in violence are not really part of movements for social and environmental justice or for political and economic democracy. The violent protesters are said to be part of the problem, not the solution. The standard that I propose draws the line between justifiable and unjustifiable militancy at a different point: the crucial contrast is between democratic and undemocratic, not between violent and nonviolent.

The distinction between violence and nonviolence cannot be the basis for distinguishing justifiable from unjustifiable protest, because the very idea of "violence" always already presupposes some degree of unjustifiability. If I push a man to the ground to prevent him from stabbing a nearby child, I am using physical force. But am I committing an act of violence? Most of us would be reluctant to use the word in this way. In contrast, suppose that I push the same man to the ground in order to block him from accessing a building that I am picketing, in the context of a general strike. Here, many would be only too quick to reach for the word "violent"; others, still, would hesitate. Consider a third case: What if I push that same man to the ground to express my contempt for his religion? In this case, perhaps everyone would agree that this is a violent act. And yet, in all three cases I perform an act of the same type, namely, pushing a man to the ground. Why do we not describe all of these actions, or none of them, as violent? The answer is clear: we are reluctant to call any act violent if we regard it as admirable and morally sound. This is one reason why one hears so little talk of "violent self-defence." Self-defence is considered morally acceptable, so we resist describing it as violent.

The implications are both obvious and important. To ask, Is violence acceptable? is already a mistake. In effect, it amounts to asking, Is unacceptable force acceptable? Instead, we should pose questions that are far less loaded, and for this reason far more interesting: Is it acceptable to participate in a riot? When, if ever, is it defensible to use or threaten to use armed force? What about arson attacks against unoccupied buildings? Can black bloc street-fighting tactics ever be justified, and if so, under what conditions?

These questions are more challenging. It is easy to declare, in a rather self-satisfied way, that all violence is unacceptable. But as long as this is only a covert way of saying that it is unacceptable to use unacceptable force, it tells us nothing. If one were to say that it is wrong to push a man to the ground to prevent him from stabbing a child, this would at least qualify as a substantive position on a controversial question. On the other hand, it would show a rather shocking undervaluation of the importance of protecting children from physical attacks. As a practical matter, almost everyone who claims to oppose all violence would in fact support the use of physical force to repel a child's attacker. We should, therefore, regard sweeping pronouncements against all violence with a suspicious eye. For the most part, these declarations are a way of hiding the difficult questions behind a veil of superficial moral certainty. In this book, I aim to address real questions with direct, if sometimes controversial, answers that are grounded in a principled position about what makes confrontational protest – in very many cases – defensible as an aid to democracy.

I call my articulation of such a position "the democratic standard." Its aim is to vindicate the conviction that, for the most part, militant protest is good for democracy. The democratic standard has two parts. First, it offers an interpretation of the democratic ideal, which equates democracy with public autonomy, that is, the self-governance of people through inclusive, reason-guided public discussion. Second, it proposes a set of four principles of soundness, which jointly spell out when and on what basis it is consistent with the democratic ideal to set aside discussion and apply forceful pressure through adversarial, confrontational protest.

In developing this standard, I have drawn together two strands of my own background. On the one hand, I am a long-time social activist, shaped by my participation in grassroots social movements, including the Occupy movement and other experiences of popular resistance. These experiences have helped me to appreciate the importance of assembly democracy and the building of grassroots social power outside of and often in direct opposition to the institutions of the official political process. On the other hand, I am an academic political philosopher, specializing in normative democratic theory. The conception of democracy proposed in this book, which I call autonomous democracy, is a kind of anticapitalist radicalization of a view that has gained wide acceptance among democratic theorists today, "deliberative democracy." This is the view that democratic legitimacy is a function not so much of voting (or of preference-counting generally), but of "voice," the capacity to raise one's concerns in a public forum and to have these concerns addressed through a deliberative process that gravitates toward consensus.[6]

The assembly democracy of the activists and the deliberative democracy of the philosophers converge on the view that a political community or social structure should be recognized as democratic to the extent that it proceeds on the basis of the self-governance of people through inclusive processes of reason-guided public discussion. In my variant of this conception of democracy, it is especially important that the authority of these discussion processes should be neither usurped by unaccountable elites nor overridden by institutions or systems of power. If intransigent elites or unresponsive institutions ignore the decisions that emerge from such discussion, thereby denying voice to many people, then democracy is fatally undermined. Democracy, according to this view, is a process of hearing stakeholders and resolving conflict through inclusive and empowered processes of collective decision-making.

Nevertheless, reality will routinely disappoint expectations founded upon this idealized conception. In practice, we can be quite sure that intransigent elites and unresponsive institutions will repeatedly stand in the way of democracy as dialogue. Politicians will often brazenly disregard public opinion, declaring that there is no alternative but to impose an unpopular but business-friendly tax policy. Corporations will often act out of shameless indifference to the public interest, appealing to the higher authority of market forces as if this were a sufficient justification for their contempt for social justice.

And this is why democratic theory needs a standard for discerning when militancy is appropriate. When, precisely out of respect for the ideal of self-governance through reason-guided public discussion, is it justified to take action on a different basis: not as partners in a deliberative process converging toward consensus, but as adversaries locked in struggle, fighting to defeat a corporation that is unmoved by the force of the better argument or a politician who refuses to listen to reason? It is this sort of guidance that the democratic standard is designed to offer: guidance about when and on what basis one might sometimes be entitled, or even obligated, to adopt a course of militant resistance, when reason-guided discussion alone is helpless in the face of unreasonable power.

At the heart of the democratic standard lies a set of four principles. These criteria can be used to determine when militancy is consistent with democracy, and what kinds of militancy are consistent with democracy in specific contexts. The principles are explained in detail in chapter three, but for now, I will confine myself to bluntly stating them:

1. *Opportunity Principle:* Militancy should create new opportunities to resolve substantive and pressing grievances, when attempts to do so through reason-guided public discussion are thwarted by intransigent elites or unresponsive institutions.
2. *Agency Principle:* Militancy should encourage the most directly affected people to take the lead in securing the resolution of their own grievances.
3. *Autonomy Principle:* Militancy should enhance the power of people to govern themselves through inclusive, reason-guided public discussion.

4. *Accountability Principle:* Militancy should limit itself to acts that can be defended publicly, plausibly, and in good faith as duly sensitive to the democratic values of common decency and the common good.

Together with the underlying democratic ideal from which they are derived, these principles make up the democratic standard that is applied to controversial cases of militancy in this book.

When an act of militant protest meets the tests set out by the democratic standard, that act may be said to satisfy the standard, that is, to be justifiable in democratic terms as a case of sound militancy. A general strike, called in response to indifference or intransigence on the part of the powerful, in order to address serious grievances after nonconfrontational efforts have fallen flat, may satisfy the opportunity principle quite well. If it is led by the most affected people, undertakes to establish public assemblies or other forums where the issues can be openly debated and decisions taken, and engages in tactics that are publicly defensible in terms of the dignity of each (common decency) and the welfare of all (the common good), then it would likely also satisfy the agency, autonomy, and accountability principles.

Some cases of militant protest may stray from the path set out by these principles. The militant action in question may predictably make resolving the grievance less likely, rather than more likely (so that it fails to live up to an expectation implicit in the opportunity principle). Or the way the action is carried out could weaken popular autonomy and strengthen the hand of the very elites or systems of power that are blocking popular empowerment (which clashes with a requirement of the autonomy principle). In these cases, the democratic standard encourages us to be wary, or, depending on the degree to which the action runs afoul of the standard, critical or even hostile. Hopefully, the standard can also offer guidance about how the action could be re-oriented toward a better alignment with the democratic ideal.

I will argue that almost every form of militancy, from classical, nonviolent civil disobedience to armed struggle, at least sometimes satisfies the democratic standard and deserves admiration, but that no form of militancy always satisfies it. So, while I attempt to show that, in general terms, militant protest is good for democracy, I make no attempt to suggest that militancy is always justifiable in this way. Instead, I argue that militancy can be justified in democratic terms as long as the occasions for it, and the forms taken by it, are chosen in ways that are consistent with the democratic ideal. Then, and only then, can we fully embrace militancy as a language of the unheard and a marker of civic virtue.[7]

These normative principles try to thread the needle between two seemingly conflicting imperatives. On the one hand, political action should be informed by and faithful to the democratic ideal, with its preference for reason-guided discussion and consensus-building. On the other hand, political action should also be realistic enough to remain effective when elites or institutions persistently act to subvert that ideal. The principles I propose attempt to be sensitive to both imperatives at once: they encourage a willingness to use confrontation when elites and systems of power are indifferent to reasons and arguments, but they steer activists toward occasions for militancy, and forms of militancy, that remain faithful to democratic notions of self-governance, popular empowerment, and public justification. In this way, the militant protester can serve as a tribune of democracy – a defender of the self-governance of people against threats or barriers to democratization posed by elites and systems that lack the militant's commitment to public autonomy and public reason.

In Part I of this book, my concerns are general and foundational. I offer a broad account of militancy as an aid to democracy and a principled response to the intransigence of elites and the unresponsiveness of institutions to the public interest, and I develop an understanding of militancy as a civic virtue and a contribution to democratic politics. In Part II, I apply this understanding of admirable militancy to a wide range of protest styles, ranging from the nonviolent civil disobedience promoted by Gandhi and King to the armed insurgency promoted by Germany's Red Army Faction and other urban guerrilla groups.

The picture of militant protest that emerges is ultimately a balanced one. It encourages the embracing of many forms of militancy as contributions to democratic politics. But it also encourages holding fast to militancy's roots in the democratic impulses of people in revolt, rather than fetishizing it as an all-purpose approach to political action. If militancy is good for democracy, it is because of its sometimes-crucial role in facilitating the self-activity and self-organization of ignored or silenced people who rightly insist on being heard.

{ Part I }

A Standard of Sound Militancy

{ One }

The Militant's Vocation

"HERE, THE PEOPLE RULE, and the government obeys." This declaration is posted on signs marking off areas controlled by the Zapatista movement of Indigenous rebellion in parts of rural Chiapas, Mexico.[1] In Chiapas, where rebel-held areas are administered by a system of grassroots good-governance councils outside the control of the Mexican state, this insistence on popular self-rule has a directly practical significance. But for most of us, it remains an ideal: the democratic ideal, that the people should be autonomous or self-governing.

The reality we face is all too often starkly different. Elites in government and business routinely ignore the will of the people, and often exercise their power with brazen disregard for the public interest. When critics raise objections, elites reply with the now-familiar declaration of intransigence: There is no alternative! The relentless pressures of the new global economy, they say, enforce a regime of strict subservience on the part of legislators and the public to the priorities of corporations, bankers, and investors. In this new order, it seems, the people cannot dictate; they can only accept. The situation has been aptly described as the onset of a "post-democratic era."[2]

And yet, there are those who reject this narrowing down of politics into obedience. Instead of answering the demand to obey with grudging or resigned compliance, they respond with defiant displays of refusal: civil disobedience, general strikes, riots, and other forms of adversarial confrontation. In late 2011, for example, farmers in the province of Guangdong in southern China "besieged government buildings, attacked police officers and overturned SWAT team vehicles during protests . . . against the seizure of farmland."[3] Earlier that year, in Madison, Wisconsin, thousands of public sector workers poured into the State Capitol building to protest an anti-union law, with many refusing to leave the building for weeks in "one of the largest labor mobilizations in the U.S. in a generation."[4] In early 2013, "hundreds of women" in rural India "clashed with police" while "locked in a bitter battle with the state government" of Odisha over plans to displace the villagers for the sake of an industrial construction project.[5] In all of these cases, the message of the protesters is the same: Here, the people rule.

Some observers are sure that we should admire these resisters, seeing in them what Martin Luther King saw in the militants of his own time: "stalwart fighters for democracy."[6] These sympathetic observers draw inspiration from the resisters' courage and determination, and want more people to emulate their unruly forms of engagement. There are others, however, who draw the opposite conclusion: they regard the rebels with suspicion, noting that they seem unwilling to accept the inevitable. Their militancy is irrational, these critics complain, because the protesters resist even when they are informed by the experts that resistance is futile. Before settling on one view or the other, let's examine the role these militant protesters play in public affairs today.

In this chapter, I first explore two case studies in the recent history of militancy – the Assemblies movement of the past few years and the Global Justice movement from around the turn of the twenty-first century. I examine the concerns and impulses that animate present-day militants, and underline the extent to which popular empowerment is central to their aims and methods. Second, I draw on King's thinking to develop a sophisticated account of the nature of militancy. My hope is that this account will be broadly acceptable to readers, regardless of where they stand on the political spectrum. I avoid a conception of militancy that prejudges the controversial questions that I will take up in later chapters by introducing loaded definitions or inflammatory terms like "violence" and "terror." Instead, I aim to develop a vocabulary for debating the issues that could be accepted by all, regardless of their positions on particular controversial questions. This vocabulary is meant to illuminate rather than prejudice the debates that so often swirl around militancy today.

The Assemblies Movement: From the Arab Spring to Occupy and Beyond

At the end of 2011, *Time* created something of a stir when it named "The Protester" as its Person of the Year.[7] Of course, it was not meant to be a favourable judgment about the merits of protest and rebellion. It was simply an acknowledgement that the preceding year had witnessed the most dramatic global upsurge of popular rebellion and militant street protest since the late 1960s.

The "year of the protester" began in early January, when Mohamed Bouazizi, a street vendor in Tunisia, killed himself by self-immolation to express his indignation at the harassment and extortion to which he had been subjected by public officials. His tragic action proved to be a catalyst for an escalating wave of street protests in Tunisia that eventually toppled the government and sent deposed president Zine al-Abidine Ben Ali fleeing into exile.[8] In itself, this would have been a historic achievement for The Protester. But the Tunisian revolution also set an example for nearby countries in North Africa and the Middle East. Long-simmering discontent in Egypt soon turned to open revolt, including sustained mass protest and a wave of strikes, amid demands that the president, Hosni Mubarak, also step down. In downtown Cairo, a new element was introduced, which would prove decisive in the coming months: an occupation of Tahrir Square in the city centre, where daily public assemblies were held to conduct debates on how to move the revolution forward. A journalist describes how these assemblies worked:

> In Tahrir, the square that has become the focal point for the nationwide struggle against Mubarak's three-decade dictatorship, [small] groups of protesters have been debating what their precise goals

> should be. . . . Delegates from these mini-gatherings then come together to discuss the prevailing mood, before potential demands are read out over the square's makeshift speaker system. The adoption of each proposal is based on the proportion of cheers or boos it receives from the crowd at large.[9]

If any of the Egyptian protesters had expected to see a discussion or dialogue with the Mubarak regime, they quickly learned that this would not be possible. Attempting to disperse the crowd, government-organized thugs attacked the Tahrir protest with horse and camel charges, armed with whips, clubs, and guns. In the prolonged street-fighting that followed this and other attacks, the Tahrir protesters held their ground and the occupation of the square continued. As the movement spread across the country, and the tactics of occupations, marches, and strikes strengthened the hand of the revolutionaries and weakened Mubarak's grip on power, elites in the military lost confidence in the president's ability to outlast the protests. By February 11, 2011, Mubarak followed in Ben Ali's footsteps, resigning in disgrace.[10] Later he was arrested and put on trial, only to be released in the wake of the military coup of July 2013. In the years since his overthrow, Mubarak's civilian and military successors have proved, perhaps predictably, similarly reluctant to allow the people to govern themselves.

Nevertheless, the ousting of Mubarak in Egypt added momentum to the wider Arab Spring revolt, which encouraged outbursts of popular rebellion across the region, spawning revolution in Yemen, civil war in Libya, and waves of mass protest in several countries, including Algeria, Jordan, Morocco, and Bahrain.

The contagion proved hard to contain even to the broad North African and Middle Eastern region, and it soon spread across the Mediterranean, where workers, students, and the unemployed in Southern Europe took up the North African example. In Greece and Spain, anti-austerity protests began to imitate not only the mass demonstrations they had witnessed in the Arab Spring, but also the tactic of occupying city squares. Like their counterparts in Cairo, the people of Madrid, Barcelona, Athens, and Thessaloniki, calling themselves the "Indignados," used the squares they occupied as outposts of popular self-rule; at each site they established a makeshift "assembly-based, consensus-seeking" democratic decision-making process.[11]

With the Arab Spring spilling over into the Indignado summer, 2011 was shaping up to be quite a year for The Protester. By the late summer, it was already possible to see the outlines of a transnational movement of people's assemblies, reflected in a revival of interest in participatory democracy and the emergence of networking websites like takethesquare.net and peoplesassemblies.org. And in a development that few saw coming, the wave of revolt surged across the Atlantic into the very heart of capitalism, as another square was occupied: Zuccotti Park, near Wall Street, in the financial district of Manhattan. By this time, protesters knew exactly how to proceed: claim public space, reject the rule of elites, and institute popular self-rule by democratic assembly, both as a way to co-ordinate the resistance and as a promissory note, indicating that another, more democratic world was indeed possible.

The Occupy Wall Street protest added more fuel to the fire, and soon parks and squares in hundreds of cities around the world were reclaimed by protest encampments, replicating the core features of the Occupy model: first, grassroots decommodification, in which food, clothing, shelter, and cultural products were removed from the market and shared freely on the basis of need, rather than ability to pay; second, solidaristic mobilization, in which everyone marched in support of the particular demands and struggles of each movement with a presence in the camps; and third, jurisdictional contestation, as the participatory General Assemblies in each encampment took charge of a reclaimed public space and replaced the law and order of the capitalist state, now openly defied, with prefigurations of a new order, aspiring to invent new forms of equality and solidarity.[12]

Within a matter of weeks, a vast network of grassroots, working-class public assemblies had been launched, stretching across multiple continents, founded upon a common rejection of elite governance and a shared insistence that, even if only in a single park or square, here and now the people would rule.

The broader cycle of struggle associated with the Assemblies movement extended beyond these examples. The Wisconsin State Capitol occupation was followed by the launch of a Wisconsin People's Assembly in April 2011. Later in the year, climate justice protesters carried out a wave of civil disobedience against tar sands pipeline infrastructure that saw over 1,200 people arrested outside of the White House over a two-week period.[13] In the province of Quebec, postsecondary students launched an "unlimited student strike," effectively shutting down schools across the province for six full months during 2012 and defeating a government proposal to raise tuition.[14] The student strike was organized by means of weekly campus-based assemblies, which approved the strike initially and continued to meet regularly to reaffirm that support and to give political direction and instructions to spokespeople and organizers.[15] By the end of the strike, these assemblies had spread off-campus, into neighbourhood assemblies that drew nonstudents into active participation in the movement.[16]

In each case, notably, the recourse to militancy was a direct response to the recognition that the voices of the people had gone unheard, that the political process was ignoring the "the 99%" and serving only "the 1%." In most cases, this concern to find a voice and gain a hearing was reflected not only in confrontation with the authorities, but also in the setting up of radically democratic public assemblies, in which in principle everyone could come forward and speak, with the promise that finally someone would listen. In Cairo's Tahrir Square, in Athens's Syntagma Square, in New York's Zuccotti Park, and in dozens of schools and neighbourhoods across Quebec, to mention only a few examples, popular assemblies were established with a mandate to be exactly what the official political process was not: a forum where all could be heard and be taken seriously, and where – according to the hopes of many participants, at least – the only power exercised would be the power to convince one's peers by reason-giving and discussion.

The Battle of Seattle: "This is what democracy looks like!"

The Arab Spring, Indignado, and Occupy protests did much to deepen and transform the understanding of democratic politics among millions of people. In this respect, the Assemblies movement recalled an earlier outbreak of exhilarating and transnationally contagious militancy. The November 1999 protest against the World Trade Organization (WTO), in Seattle, Washington, was at the time a crucial turning point for North American radicals. Along with the series of high-profile global justice summit protests that followed over the subsequent two years, it fundamentally reconfigured their picture of what democracy looks like.

On the morning of November 30, 1999, tens of thousands of protesters poured into Seattle's streets, with the declared aim of stopping the unstoppable, reversing the irreversible, and demanding an alternative to the globalized capitalism to which no alternative was supposed to be possible. They must have surprised even themselves when they were able to gain an unqualified victory in this epic Battle of Seattle, as it was soon dubbed. Yet they did exactly what they had said they would do. Filling the streets, blocking intersections, and fighting back in the face of relentless, lawless police violence, the Seattle protesters shut down the ministerial meetings of the WTO, derailing an elite negotiating process that had been months in the making. In so doing, they sent a message that the emerging Global Justice movement was capable of mounting a real political challenge to the neoliberal agenda of corporate globalization, even in the absence of any significant support for the movement's anticorporate politics among the major political parties in any of the affluent countries. In North America, as in Western Europe, political elites had long ago settled upon a consensus agenda of business-friendly "free market" globalization, a policy framework promoted and enforced by the WTO.

In Seattle, the protesters imposed a humiliating tactical defeat on the rich and the powerful. They did this not in spite of but because of their militancy and their lack of any ties to the politicians, bureaucrats, and business leaders who jointly run the WTO. In this way, they showed that what the Indigenous people had done in Mexico in 1994,[17] what striking trade union militants had done in South Korea in 1997,[18] and what the workers and students of France had done in 1995[19] could also be done in the United States of America: militant struggles, drawing in thousands of participants, could generate enough social power to force governments and corporations into retreat. But could others, following these examples, take things still further, winning not just a battle but the whole war against social and environmental injustice, against political and economic plutocracy? Could activists actually win the kind of global alternative to corporate capitalism that was supposed to be inconceivable?

The electric appeal of this thought gave Seattle a special meaning, particularly for North American radicals, at the turn of the millennium. Seattle meant that mass public protest could be effective in ways that had rarely been imagined by activists in the neoliberal era. Protest could be symbolic, to be sure; it could make a point. But now it was becoming apparent – as though through the glimmer of a long-forgotten lesson – that resistance could also be transformative. Its power could rival the power of corporations and governments; it could change the course of history.

Just as important was what Seattle taught many thousands of activists about democracy: that democracy was not primarily, perhaps not at all, about citizens choosing among candidates in elections or about politicians holding votes in legislatures. The recurring chant of the Seattle protesters – "This is what democracy looks like!" – was taken quite literally by many radical activists. The WTO ministerial meetings, with their closed-door negotiations; their exclusion of stakeholders other than corporate CEOs, industry lobbyists, and government officials; and their encirclement by metal fences and brutal riot police embodied everything that was undemocratic, indeed antidemocratic, about corporate globalization. And the protesters, orchestrating the defeat of this antidemocratic force by means of a global popular revolt from below, had assumed the mantle of the people's tribune: the upholder of democracy's deepest meaning and its highest potential. The protests themselves had been organized in a spirit of radically democratic, horizontal inclusiveness, in a system of spokescouncils that tried to give a voice to every self-organized affinity group participating in the action.[20]

The Seattle example was soon imitated – or discovered independently in the wake of similarly inspiring achievements in other places – by millions of activists around the world. As the movement gained momentum, mass protests were held in April 2000 in Washington, DC, against the International Monetary Fund (IMF); in Melbourne, in September 2000, against the World Economic Forum; in Prague that same month, against the IMF and World Bank; in Quebec City, in April 2001, against a summit to negotiate a Free Trade Area of the Americas; in Genoa, in July 2001, against a meeting of the G8 heads of government; and so on.

After the terrorist attacks of September 11, 2001, the movement lost much of its momentum, eventually morphing into an antiwar movement that drew millions of people into the streets worldwide, deterring some governments from joining the rush to war, but ultimately failing to prevent war's onset altogether. By then, however, a crucial learning process had already taken place. The lesson of Seattle and the other global justice protests – that democracy is not equivalent to electoral politics, but instead means, much more fundamentally, the power of the people – meant that the movement had deepened the analysis and broadened the horizons of a generation of activists.[21]

Voice to the Voiceless

These two case studies tie together some key episodes in the recent history of militancy. Outbreaks of confrontation like the Arab Spring and the Battle of Seattle suggest not so much what militancy is usually like, but what it aspires to be at its best. In particular, these case studies highlight the special importance of democracy in the self-understanding of the militant resister. In slogans like "Here, the people rule" and "This is what democracy looks like!" and in practices like the popular assemblies of Tahrir Square or Zuccotti Park and the spokescouncils of the Seattle protest, the high points of militancy offer clues to what I call the militant's vocation or proper function. They reveal what the militant is trying to do, or rather, to be.

Martin Luther King may have offered the most vivid and concise depiction of this vocation when he suggested that the militant aspires "to give a voice to the voiceless."[22] But there is an important distinction between giving a voice to and being the voice of the voiceless. When it is done well, militancy does not usurp the voice or the agency of the silenced and ignored. It does not claim to speak on behalf of others. On the contrary, militancy ushers the unheard directly onto centre stage, offering them a language, a vehicle to make themselves heard. Militancy is a form of engagement by which the unheard make themselves impossible to ignore.

To the militant, democracy is not about unobstructed rule by elected politicians. That is a police officer's view of democracy: democracy as the enforcement of the commands handed down by legislators. Militant protesters, as King said, are "stalwart fighters for democracy," but most of their fights are waged *against* governments and elected officials. Often the only way to fight for democracy is by refusing to obey the law, by attempting to "dislocate the functioning of a city,"[23] and in general by instigating confrontations with the powerful.

Militancy normally arises in response to patterns of persistent insensitivity to the concerns of certain classes and categories of people – the exploited, the excluded, the oppressed. Lacking access to positions of power and status, or the wealth and influence needed to steer social structures and systems to their own advantage, these groups' expressions of dissent are routinely ignored. They can protest in the conventional, officially authorized ways, but too often such gestures are fruitless. They can write a letter to a public official, or sign a petition, or march calmly in the street, seeking redress for important and pressing grievances. But the powerful find it all too easy to ignore these voices of powerless complaint. In this context, the militant's proper function is to press past the limits set by the official political process. If a petition is ignored, why not block traffic on a highway or a bridge? If voting in an election is inconsequential or if sending a letter to a public official is ineffective, what about a riot or a general strike? What about disrupting a business or defying the police or the courts? This may be the kind of insistent and unruly civic engagement that the powerful cannot ignore. Indeed, even within social movements, unruliness and confrontational action by marginalized groups is often needed to ensure that struggles are genuinely inclusive and that all participants can have their voices heard and their autonomy respected.

King's wording also points us in the direction of a richer understanding of the democratic ideal. In this conception, democracy is not primarily a matter of voting, or the expression of public choice through preference-counting. Instead, it is mainly a matter of voice, or the empowerment of people to govern themselves through inclusive, reason-guided public discussion. This conception of voice has been given its most systematic and rigorous articulation by German-American economist Albert O. Hirschman, in his influential book, *Exit, Voice, and Loyalty*.[24] I delve more deeply into Hirschman's work in chapter eight. Here I only want to note that, like Hirschman, I understand voice to mean access to opportunities to make oneself heard within an organization or association, and the corresponding capacity to influence decisions and outcomes by offering input that is taken seriously and regarded as important.[25] It is the denial of voice in this sense that militancy attempts to overcome.

Voting can sometimes play an important role in communicating popular preferences. But authentic democracy is more about public autonomy than public choice, which can often be extracted under threat. The popular will communicated in a voting process may simply reflect a preexisting imbalance of power, which effectively intimidates the vulnerable. We are only too familiar with the constant threats from investors to withdraw capital, and thereby to kill jobs, if the people ever dare to demand egalitarian, redistributive public policies. The demand for public autonomy is democratic in a much richer sense than mere public choice. Public autonomy requires that the people dictate the terms of social co-operation based on a broadly shared understanding of the common good and the requirements of justice, after a thorough process of inclusive, wide-ranging discussion. Public autonomy, in this more demanding sense, means genuine self-rule.

Although this understanding of democracy may seem to be closely tied to the consensus-oriented assembly democracy of the Occupy movement, it is by no means a new idea. Already in the nineteenth century, Karl Marx, for one, affirmed this conception of democratic rule, calling it "government of the people by the people."[26] Drawing inspiration from the political practice of the Haudenosaunee Confederacy, which he treated as the most advanced form of democracy in modern times, Marx thought that achieving public autonomy would require a community-based, participatory form of self-rule through inclusive discussion. "Supreme authority," he said, would be vested in a "Council," operating as "a democratic assembly, [in which] every adult male [and] female member had a voice upon all questions brought before it."[27] Marx, like King, chose to describe democracy in terms of voice: every male and female member would have "a voice upon all questions." One can recognize in Marx's ideal, modelled on his understanding of Haudenosaunee horizontalism, the participatory and egalitarian style of democracy embraced by the assemblies in Cairo, Athens, and Zuccotti Park, and by the spokescouncils of the Global Justice movement.[28]

Obviously, the idea of democracy as public autonomy is a normative ideal, not an empirical description of how the world works. Because reasonable discussion is often helpless in the face of unreasonable power, militancy steps forward, to push back against power and money on behalf of democracy. Militancy encounters and confronts the unreasonableness of power in two basic forms, which Chalmers Johnson in his book *Revolutionary Change* calls "elite intransigence" and "social systems" that are unresponsive to popular grievances.[29] Modifying his formulations, I refer mainly to intransigent elites and unresponsive systems of power.

This, then, is the militant's vocation: to push against these barriers to break the grip of the heteronomy, or rule by others, that blocks the path to "government of the people by the people." As stalwart fighters for democracy, militants defend public autonomy against the threats posed to it by the powerful.

This book explores the ethics and politics of militancy, and seeks to vindicate the militant's vocation in the face of critics who object to a recourse to forceful pressure. For the most part, it is a book about what militancy ought to be. At the centre of my analysis of the ethics and politics of militant resistance is a normative ideal of democratic militancy as a civic virtue. But, before an ideal of militancy can be meaningfully explored, it is necessary to develop a definition of the word "militancy" and a basic vocabulary for discussing it.

What Is Militancy?

To develop such a vocabulary, I turn to Martin Luther King, from whom I borrow both the title of this book and its guiding idea, that militant resistance in its many forms endows our public life with languages of the unheard, or opportunities for the silenced and the ignored to secure a voice and gain a hearing. King not only admired but also identified with militancy. In his famous 1963 speech to the March on Washington, he spoke glowingly of "the marvellous new militancy" of the Civil Rights struggle of those years. Praising its responsiveness to what he called "the fierce urgency of Now," he contrasted militancy favourably with "the tranquillizing drug of gradualism" that continued to plague the more reformist wing of the movement.[30] It was "magnificent," he said, to see so many people in the struggle who were "determined to be free and . . . militant enough to stand up" for that freedom.[31] King was one of the most perceptive and sophisticated observers of the protest culture of his time, so it is no surprise that in his speeches and writings he highlights a number of features of militant resistance that jointly comprise the core elements of militancy.

King singles out four features of militant protest as particularly important. First, he depicts militancy as grievance-motivated: "this sweltering summer of . . . legitimate discontent will not pass," he insists, "until there is an invigorating autumn of freedom and equality."[32] Second, he depicts it as a type of adversarial action, a struggle against opponents whose intransigence blocks the resolution of such grievances: "We know through painful experience that freedom is never voluntarily given by the oppressor; it must be demanded by the oppressed."[33] Third, King depicts militancy as less a form of communication or self-expression than a form of challenge or confrontation: it "seeks to create such a crisis and establish such creative tension that a community that has constantly refused to negotiate is forced to confront the issue."[34] And finally, he depicts militant protest as a kind of collective action: militancy, King suggests, presupposes that a group of people, acting in concert, have resolved "to struggle together, to go to jail together, to stand up for freedom together."[35]

Taking note of these four elements, a rather concise definition suggests itself: "militancy" means *grievance-motivated, adversarial, and confrontational collective action.*

Let's look at each part of this definition, starting with the idea that militancy must be grievance-motivated. If I block traffic to annoy my neighbours, or to express my disappointment after the loss of a playoff game, then my actions cannot qualify as militant, whatever else one might call them. Even if I take the opportunity to throw a brick through the window of a nearby retail store, I remain outside the realm of militant action. I might be called many things after such an outburst, but no one would think to call me militant. What is missing is the motive. Militancy is a way of pressing a grievance, that is, it is a type of protest. It matters not just what I do or what effect my action has, but also, crucially, what motivates me to act as I do. There has to be a grievance that spurs me to resist, even if it is not my own grievance but that of others in solidarity with whom I have decided to act.

Next, militancy proceeds from an adversarial stance. If, motivated by some grievance, I undertake an act of protest with the intention of winning over the target of the protest (not to be confused with the audience of onlookers), acting on the assumption that they are open to reason and could well be convinced to see the soundness of my grievance, then I may be protesting, but my protest would not be militant. Militants act under the assumption that the target of their protest is intransigent and unresponsive to evidence-based arguments and rational persuasion. They treat the target of their resistance as an adversary, to be defeated in struggle or at least to be forced into retreat or pressured into making concessions.

In principle, though, even an adversarial protest could eschew confrontation. It could pursue a course of what some call "exodus" or "flight": a strategy of disengagement from the institutions deemed intransigent or unresponsive.[36] A group of workers, motivated by unfair pay and conditions and convinced that their employer could never be persuaded to treat them with fairness, could decide to quit their jobs en masse and launch a workers' co-operative. This might be radical, in one way, but it stops short of militancy. Militancy seeks out direct conflict. Adversarial acts of protest are not militant unless they are also confrontational.

The final element of the definition identifies militancy as a type of collective action. If an individual lashes out against an oppressor by exacting personal revenge – in an adversarial, confrontational way, in response to a grievance – we might well want to call this an act of rebellion or resistance. But militancy is a more specific sort of resistance. It is a way of conducting a social struggle, more or less in concert with others. It is a type of social or collective action. Individuals may be said to perform militant actions on their own, as long as they do so in the context of and as part of a wider social struggle or movement. When Rosa Parks was jailed for defying the law and a police officer's order by refusing to surrender her seat on a bus to a white passenger, for example, she undertook this action partly in her capacity as an antiracist organizer (for the local chapter of the NAACP) and a participant in the Civil Rights movement.[37] This can clearly be considered as a form of collective action, consistent with the definition.

These four salient features seem to me to form the basis for a flexible, relatively uncontroversial understanding of the concept of militancy, which ought to be acceptable both to those who attack militancy and to those who celebrate it. From here on, then, my use of the word "militancy" should be taken to mean grievance-motivated, adversarial, and confrontational collective action. At times, I condense this unwieldy formula into "confrontational protest."

Four Styles of Militancy

It is also important to develop a differentiated understanding of the ways in which particular styles of militant resistance diverge from one another. Not all militancy is alike, and different varieties raise a range of moral and political questions. Armed struggle, for instance, introduces issues that general strikes may not bring up, notably the legitimacy of physically harming or killing other people, or indeed of failing to do so where lives could have been saved by the timely deployment of armed force.

Often, people try to shed light on such differences by describing the contrast in quantitative terms, as a difference of more or less militancy. In the 1960s, they say, the Black Panther Party was more militant than the Congress on Racial Equality; in the early twentieth century, the Industrial Workers of the World union was more militant than affiliates of the American Federation of Labor. This quantitative framing of differences does capture something important, namely, that some tactics (taking up arms, for instance) look like an escalation compared to others (such as holding marches). But on closer examination, this way of putting the point turns out to be vague and misleading. Does it really make sense to say that breaking windows is more militant (or indeed less militant) than organizing a general strike? Do we really want to say that carrying a gun is more or less militant than standing in front of a tank and refusing to move aside?

The utility of such quantitative contrasts breaks down when applied to cases where the tactics differ qualitatively. To the extent that different outbreaks of confrontational resistance deploy qualitatively different tactics, we should distinguish them in ways that are illuminating and precise. For example, general strikes, which can shut down production and hence block profit making, are arguably more threatening to elites than breaking the windows of retail stores, which only forces employers to instruct their employees to fill out the appropriate insurance forms. Here the way to put the point is that general strikes are more threatening (not more militant) than window-breaking. On the other hand, breaking windows creates a more spectacular impression in the news media than picket lines do. So here we should say that window-breaking is more spectacular or more dramatic than a general strike.

Because the most important differences between forms of protest are qualitative, not quantitative, I find it helpful to analyze confrontational protest as falling into several broad types, or styles, of militancy.[38] I distinguish four basic styles, each of which can be given either a symbolic or a material application. I call them defiance, disruption, destruction, and armed force.

Defiance

In a defiant style of militancy, the resister targets some type of achieved, ascribed, or claimed authority, by refusing to recognize it or defer to it. Defiance is a type of confrontational refusal, which attempts to undermine or weaken the hold of authority, either by symbolic or by material means.

In its symbolic variant, defiance takes the form of gestures of nonrecognition, as when US antiwar protesters during the Vietnam War era staged public draft-card burnings; or when Buddhist monks in Burma staged long silent marches in 2007 in defiance of legal orders declaring these marches to be illegal; or when, beginning in 1977, the Mothers of the Plaza de Mayo in Argentina stood defiantly in a public square dressed in mourning clothes to mark their rejection of the dictatorship that abducted, tortured, and often killed their children.

In its material variant, defiance switches from gestures of nonrecognition to attempts to physically contest the capacity of an authority to impose its rule, as when black bloc protesters challenge the claim of the police to control the streets, or when troops refuse to follow orders or even turn their weapons on their officers. In both symbolic and material defiance, however, the basic intent is the same: to undercut the authority of institutions that claim the capacity or the right to dictate to others.

Disruption

In the disruptive style, protesters target not the recognition of authority, but the functioning of institutions or systems. Even a system that is not recognized as an authority may still be able to function in accordance with its own systemic imperatives. A market, for instance, or a system of transportation, administration, or criminal punishment, may be able to exercise power even over people who insistently refuse to recognize the system's legitimacy. Disruption attempts to interrupt the orderly processes of an institution or system, so that, at least for a period of time, that system cannot effectively function. The intention, usually, is to change the incentives that dictate the behaviour of elites, so that they no longer benefit from silencing or ignoring exploited, oppressed, or excluded people, but have a new incentive to take these people's grievances seriously or at least to behave differently. Workers might withdraw their labour to shut down a business, protesters might occupy the office of public officials to prevent them from carrying out their jobs, or sit-ins might disrupt retail stores or bank branches from conducting their normal business activities.

When disruption is designed to send a message, it is symbolic; when it is designed to exert forceful pressure directly, it is material. The fullest expression of disruption, however, goes beyond trying to pressure elites and establishment institutions or systems; it takes the further step of trying to destroy those elites or systems altogether, bringing them to their knees once and for all. Indeed, revolutionary strategies often give pride of place to disruptive tactics, especially to what Polish socialist Rosa Luxemburg called "the mass strike," a tactic central to both anarcho-syndicalist and Marxist strategies.[39]

Destruction

A third style of militancy targets property or other material objects for damage or destruction. Destructive protesters might destroy cars, break windows, sabotage construction machines, or burn down a laboratory or a factory. Symbolic destruction burns or smashes something to express an idea or make a point. It might, for instance, be used to destroy a statue that is deemed to celebrate a racist or imperialist figure, such as Christopher Columbus; destruction of the statue represents an expression of contempt for what he represents. The intent of material destruction is quite different. It usually targets a building or a machine that has some purpose, so that destroying it prevents that purpose from being carried out.

Although there is a lot of debate over whether or not property destruction of these kinds is "violent," this is a distraction from more important issues, notably, whether it makes good strategic sense and whether it is morally and politically justified. Everyone agrees that sometimes property should be destroyed, for example, by kicking in the locked door of a house that's on fire to rescue unconscious residents. The question is, When, if ever, should we regard confrontational protest as an appropriate, justified occasion to destroy property, and when, if ever, should we regard it as an improper or illegitimate one?

Armed Force

The final style of militancy is the use of armed force, or as it is called on the left, armed struggle. In this style, militancy takes on a paramilitary aspect, using weaponry to threaten, maim, or kill people in order to press a grievance and effect change. Often, the term "violence" is used interchangeably with "armed force." But a tactic could be violent in one sense, namely, by using physical force, without being armed; and a tactic could be armed, without being violent in any familiar sense. When the Black Panther Party conducted an armed march into the California State Assembly in 1967, they were armed but nonviolent (by any definition).[40] And when six of the participants in the 1992 Los Angeles Rebellion kicked and beat a transport worker almost to death, they were by all accounts acting violently but remained unarmed.[41] Armed force, as I use the term, is the deployment of weapons to threaten or kill people as a means of struggle. In effect, it is resistance of a military or paramilitary type.

Symbolic armed force chooses targets for communicative or expressive reasons, to send a message or score a propaganda victory. At the time of the 1979 assassination by the Irish Republican Army (Provisional IRA) of

Lord Louis Mountbatten – a relative of the British Queen – Mountbatten was not an important military target. But he symbolized colonialism and the monarchy, and his killing conveyed the idea that the IRA had the capacity to strike at high-level targets. As this example shows, symbolic armed force is no less real because its targets are chosen for propagandistic reasons.

By contrast, a material use of armed force chooses targets with a military objective in mind, such as driving an adversary out of a certain area, or raising the cost (in blood or treasure) of maintaining some policy or practice opposed by the armed resisters. The military assault on January 1, 1994, by the Zapatista Army of National Liberation (Ejército Zapatista de Liberación Nacional, or EZLN) on several towns in Chiapas, Mexico, for example, was designed to drive out Mexican military and state institutions from the region. This measure succeeded briefly, before a largely successful mid-January counteroffensive by the government to retake rebel-held towns, which forced the Zapatistas to retreat into rural areas of Chiapas where the movement has been able to retain autonomy to a considerable degree.

Practically Sound or Unsound Protest

With a definition of militancy in hand, along with a differentiated analysis of four styles of militant resistance, we are ready to get to the heart of the matter. "Militancy" is *grievance-motivated, adversarial, and confrontational collective action, aiming to give a voice to the voiceless by deploying means such as defiance, disruption, destruction, or armed force.* This account of militancy's nature has been developed specifically to avoid prejudging whether, and when, it is something to admire or to condemn. But that was a temporary measure, to set the stage for this book's central question: How can we tell the difference between militancy done well and militancy done poorly?

Some will object to this aim. Who has a right to judge how people resist their own oppression or exploitation? There is a grain of truth in this objection, but in its nihilistic version – which rejects moral assessment altogether – it goes too far. Indeed, one should avoid moralistic condemnation of people who struggle to free themselves from domination, even if one worries that their methods are questionable. But we can pay heed to this concern without being panicked by it. The trick is to apply morality, without succumbing to moralism; to accept the responsibility to exercise good judgment, without being judgmental.

One way to find this middle position is to choose a vocabulary that is suitably normative – that is, that guides or steers us toward acting as we should – without classifying everything in absolute terms as either right or wrong, legitimate or illegitimate. Accordingly, I opt for a normative vocabulary that is less an either/or than a more-or-less contrast, so that I can acknowledge that some militancy is far from ideal, without automatically having to repudiate it as absolutely wrong or illegitimate. The terms I will use are, unsurprisingly, drawn from King, who sometimes distinguished between "practically sound" and "practically unsound" styles of protest.[42]

This contrast between sound and unsound militancy is to be understood as a continuum, from an ideal of the most admirable militancy at one end, to the cautionary, negative examples of vicious militancy at the other. Most militancy falls somewhere between these two extremes, but I judge most justice-motivated militancy to be generally sound, even if the standard of soundness adopted in this book offers suggestions about how it could be more sound. By articulating a set of criteria, my aim is not (except in the most egregious cases) to condemn deviations from the ideal. It is to offer a standard by which to steer militancy in the right direction. Perhaps militancy almost never satisfies a standard of ideal soundness. But some cases come closer to the ideal than others do, and this awareness can help steer militancy toward better, more admirable forms and methods, so that it more fully embodies the militant's vocation to give a voice to the voiceless.

Sound militancy, in this sense, is a civic virtue. That is to say, it is a type of civic engagement that should be admired, because of its salutary effect on public affairs. But how do we know when militancy is sound? We are now ready to look at practical criteria to inform these judgments.

{ Two }

The Liberal Objection

IF MILITANCY IS A CIVIC VIRTUE that defends public autonomy, then presumably it should elicit admiration. When a crowd of feminist activists blocks traffic to protest sexual harassment of women workers, or a group of striking nurses defends a picket line against police enforcing an injunction, this behaviour should be regarded as noble and as an example to be imitated by others. Some onlookers do react in this way. But not everyone admires confrontational protesters. In fact, some people specifically dispute the claim that militancy is good for democracy. They believe, on the contrary, that militancy is a failing, either because it undermines fragile democratic institutions by eroding respect for law and order, or because it resorts to forceful pressure when reason-guided, good-faith dialogue is called for. In this chapter, I explore these concerns, focusing especially on the latter, which I call the liberal objection to militancy.

The Defence of Order

I use the label "conservative" as a shorthand way to describe those whose objection to militancy is motivated by a concern about its impact on public order and the stability and durability of what they regard as the fragile institutions of modern democracy. And these conservative critics can be especially strident in their condemnations.

To conservative critics, militancy is divisive and antisocial, its organizers are troublemakers or "outside agitators," and a forceful crackdown to reimpose law and order is a suitable response. This objection does not always arise out of scorn for the protesters' grievances. Often, it arises from the fear that protesters might undermine something of great importance to everyone. After all, justice and democracy can only flourish, in this view, in an orderly society with reliable and relatively stable traditions and institutions. But these traditions and institutions are fragile in that they depend for their survival on the willingness of successive generations to remain loyal to them and to recognize them as worth continuing over time. The militant's eagerness to defy authority, to disrupt social systems and practices, or to attack the rights of property and entrenched hierarchies seems misguided and dangerous, because it threatens to unleash disorder and social divisions that could undo the foundations of social stability and the shared sense of community. Restoring law and order by cracking down on militant protesters, therefore, is a kind of societal self-defence against a threat to the social order.

This need not be dismissed as a frivolous complaint. It starts out from the plausible assumption that a society cannot flourish without some degree of commitment among its members to a shared framework of institutions that can be widely embraced and reproduced over time. Even revolutionaries want the revolution to yield relatively stable and predictable institutions, which can enable people to plan how they hope and expect to live their lives.

Nevertheless, the objection is far from convincing. King addressed its core claim in his "Letter from a Birmingham Jail." Defending the style of militancy that I call "defiance" from conservative critics, King argued that the critics of militancy go astray because they are "more devoted to 'order' than to justice."[1] Order is indeed important, to the extent that it provides a reliable setting for the unfolding of just and democratic social relations among equals. It is not desirable to live in a chaotic, disordered mess of a society, with no functional institutions. However, the order contested by militants often guarantees the reproduction of unjust practices, relationships, and institutions. The defence of order may sometimes be important, but only when the more stringent requirement to satisfy the demands of justice is already met.

Order is secondary; it only has value when something else that is deemed valuable and worth preserving depends upon it. We welcome the orderly rules of soccer or basketball, which allow us to play the game without conflict, but the same cannot be said for orderliness in the regulations of an oppressive system, like that of male domination of women. On the contrary, disorder and disruption are desirable to impede that system's reproduction over time. As King puts it, "law and order exist for the purpose of establishing justice and . . . when they fail in this purpose they become the dangerously structured dams that block the flow of social progress."[2]

In short, King is right. We ought to be more devoted to justice than to order. An unjust order should be opposed at every opportunity, and the disorder that accompanies such opposition should trouble us less than the fact that the prevailing order now blocks the path to justice. King's argument, I take it, effectively dispenses with the conservative objection. But the liberal critic of militancy poses a much more serious challenge.

A Challenge from Within

According to the liberal objection, militancy is undemocratic because it is coercive. It resorts to forceful pressure, when the democratic ideal demands that we use reason-guided discussion to resolve our conflicts. By using confrontation instead of consensus-building and conversation, the militant crosses the line from democracy to elitism, positioning militants as a new counterelite that attempts to impose outcomes by force rather than by persuasion.

This objection is more serious for two reasons. First, whereas the conservative objection looks at the issue from the law-and-order perspective of police officers and politicians, the liberal objection looks at it from the perspective of activists who oppose elitism and authoritarianism, and who worry that militancy imports these practices into the movement from the outside. In other words, the liberal objection is a challenge from within movements that struggle for social and environmental justice, rather than a challenge emanating from adversaries of these struggles. More often than not, it is fellow activists who raise these arguments, accusing militants of undermining the struggle for justice by the methods they employ. Second, this objection does not rely on an inflated sense of the importance of order, which the militant can casually dismiss. It relies on the very value that the militant's vocation elevates to the highest importance: the value of public autonomy through inclusive, reason-guided discussion. This is a premise that the militant cannot disregard.

Indeed, paradoxically, the liberal objection shares with the partisans of militancy a similar understanding of the nature of democracy and of its role in conferring legitimacy on decisions about matters of common concern. Like the proponents of militancy who want supreme authority to rest in assemblies or councils in which each man and woman would have a voice, the liberal also wants broad-based, inclusive discussion to be the basis for public decision-making. And yet, the liberal draws from this premise an alarming conclusion: that militancy is not a civic virtue, but a vice.

Let's look at the roots of this objection. Traditionally, liberalism was suspicious of democracy in certain respects. The classical liberal political philosophers, like John Locke and Adam Smith, wanted to insulate a private sphere of property and market relations from what they regarded as the danger of public control. Later, more egalitarian liberal philosophers, like John Stuart Mill, were more accepting of an expansive role for public institutions, but still worried about "the tyranny of the majority," and reasserted in new ways the need to protect a private sphere from public control. In one of liberalism's most recent iterations, however, it has not only embraced democracy, but also articulated a conception of democracy that resonates with some themes of radical democratic theories of assembly democracy.[3] This innovation in liberal thought has taken the form of what theorists call "the deliberative turn" in democratic theory. In the past two decades, the academic discipline of democratic theory (a branch of political philosophy) has come to be dominated by a particular theoretical perspective, the deliberative theory of democratic legitimacy,[4] which underlines the value of inclusive, reason-guided public discussion.

This deliberative turn in democratic theory arose in response to some of the same frustrations that motivated the militants of the Assemblies and Global Justice movements. Like movement activists, democratic theorists have also looked with alarm at the grotesque role of big money and backroom deals in contemporary electoral politics.[5] Deliberative theory took shape as an attempt to vindicate an inspiring ideal of politics as a collaborative inquiry into the common good and the requirements of justice, in contrast to the grim reality of official politics as a vehicle for the rich and powerful to augment their advantages. Surely, the deliberative democrats insisted, there must be more to democracy than media-savvy public relations campaigns and the selling of votes by donation-hungry legislators to the highest-bidding industry lobbyists.

Essentially, the deliberative theory offers an understanding of democratic legitimacy which, like the Assemblies and Global Justice movements, proposes to treat voice rather than voting as the central feature of democratic decision-making. A decision is democratically legitimate, according to this view, only if it emerged from an inclusive process of reason-guided public discussion or "dialogical deliberation." Turkish American political philosopher Seyla Benhabib puts the point this way: "Legitimacy in complex democratic societies must be thought to result from the free and unconstrained public deliberation of all about matters of common concern." This is necessary, she writes, because a decision can only be plausibly depicted as democratically legitimate to the extent that it "can be viewed as the outcome of a procedure of free and reasoned deliberation among individuals considered as moral and political equals."[6] In the wake of this kind of inclusive rational dialogue, a vote of some sort would no doubt rightly be expected, so that this rationally determined public opinion can register its informed preference. But it is the role of inclusive rational dialogue in the formation of public preferences, not the sheer number of people holding those preferences, that confers legitimacy on decisions.

By way of informal comparison, we care what the great majority of scientists think about an issue like the evolution of species or the causes of climate change. But the reason we care is not because we are impressed by the sheer number who hold a certain view. Rather, we care what they think because of the manner in which we suppose their judgments were formed, namely, by the application of procedures of inquiry that are known to be reliable. We expect that they base their opinions on methods of exposing hypotheses to empirical testing, subjecting research to the scrutiny of peer review, and so on. The number of people holding a certain view would be irrelevant if we imagined that the process by which they formed their opinions was no more reliable than that of anyone else. In the same way, the deliberative democrat believes that we have reason to treat democratic decisions as legitimate not because they are numerically majoritarian, but because – if these decisions are indeed properly democratic – they emerge from processes of inclusive public discussion, brought about by no force but that of the better argument. If a majority preference is based on nothing more than misinformation, manipulation, or the "manufacturing of consent,"[7] according to the deliberative account, it loses its claim to legitimacy.

As an insistent demand to put reason-guided and inclusive public discussion at the centre of political life, the deliberative theory contributes to an understanding of the democratic ideal, and to a diagnosis of the democratic deficits that erode the credibility of ostensibly democratic political institutions. About this much, the deliberative democracy of this new democratic liberalism converges with the autonomous democracy of the militants of Tahrir Square and the Battle of Seattle.

However, this view can take a further step in a questionable direction. When deliberative-democratic liberals reflect on the implications of this view for evaluating militancy, they often take a stance of deep scepticism. What should one make of those militant resisters, shutting down the WTO meetings, blocking traffic on the Brooklyn Bridge, or disrupting legislative sessions of the Wisconsin State Assembly? If the deliberative conception is right, are the militant protesters not marching in the wrong direction? Should they not be endeavouring to extend, expand,

and deepen the dialogue, rather than suspending dialogue with adversaries in favour of confrontation?

The liberal concern can be framed in terms of civic virtue. The idea that the deliberative theory of democracy implies a corresponding deliberative theory of civic virtue is often only hinted at by deliberative democrats. But sometimes it is explicitly articulated. Philosopher Paul Weithman, for one, has written in virtue-ethical terms about the idea of a "deliberative character,"[8] the kind of behavioural dispositions that deliberative democracy needs people to exhibit, notably openness to giving and asking for reasons in a process of ongoing commitment to dialogue. Political theorists Amy Gutmann and Dennis Thompson, in the same vein, have tried to describe "a distinctly deliberative type of character" that "permits a democracy to flourish in the face of fundamental moral disagreement."[9] Weithman, Gutmann, and Thompson argue that people who embody the best modes of civic engagement should be willing to give reasons for the outcomes they favour, and to be responsive to the reasons given by others. The best way of being politically engaged, they suggest, is to be open to rational persuasion by strong arguments offered by those with whom one has disagreed. In short, deliberative virtue would encourage openness to reason-based arguments and willingness to enter into good-faith dialogue with one's adversaries. But crucially, this is something the militant resister – employing adversarial, confrontational action – seems unwilling to undertake.

It is easy to see how one might regard this dialogical model of civic virtue as a straightforward implication of the deliberative theory of democracy. Political decisions, according to the deliberative theory, are only legitimate if they are the outcomes of reason-guided public discussion. In turn, if conflicts between people or interest groups are to be legitimately resolved, the parties to those conflicts have to be willing to enter into such a dialogue. Those who refuse to do so stand in the way of legitimate conflict resolution and block the possibility of a democratic outcome. So the idea of deliberative virtue seems to fall right out of the deliberative theory of legitimacy. Moreover, it can be the basis for an attack on the vocation of the militant protester.

Thus, the deliberative theory of civic virtue, despite its similarity to the theory of autonomous democracy, is regarded by deliberative-democratic liberals as the ultimate basis for the liberal objection that militancy is a failing because it resorts to force when democracy demands ongoing dialogue. If militancy is to be defended as a civic virtue, a convincing response to this objection is needed. Most of militancy's defenders would probably answer with one of the three most popular justifications for militancy: amoralism, consequentialism, and pluralism.

Three Common Defences of Militancy

The Amoralist Reply

The amoralist challenges not the liberal's conception of what is virtuous, but the very idea that vice and virtue are relevant to assessing militancy. In other words, the amoralist does not object to a particular standard, such as the deliberative liberal's standard of unshakeable commitment to dialogue and rational persuasion, but rather to the application of any normative standard to resistance. Drawing on the Machiavellian notion that political action is a realm of pure strategy, the amoralist wants to drop discussion of the moral rightness of political actions and to replace it with discussion of their strategic effectiveness. Historically, perhaps the most well-known advocate for this view was Leon Trotsky, the Russian Marxist, from whom I borrow the term "amoralism."

From exile in the late 1930s, Trotsky published a text, *Their Morals and Ours*, which itself restated an argument that he had made several years earlier, in his 1920 pamphlet, *Terrorism and Communism*.[10] His presentation is rather polemical, but in one crucial passage, he spells out his position in this way: "A means can be justified only by its end. But the end in its turn needs to be justified. . . . The end is justified if it leads to increasing the power of man over nature and to the abolition of the power of man over man."[11] At first glance, this might not seem amoralist at all. After all, Trotsky specifies two normative standards, power over nature and liberation of people. But on closer inspection, he has instituted a conceptual boundary between two domains: the domain of ends, for which one fights politically, and the domain of means, which are the ways in which one fights for those ends. According to Trotsky, morality only applies to the first, not to the second, of these two domains. He is a moralist about ends, and an amoralist about means or tactics. For example, he concedes that whether or not to oppose a war is a moral question. But whether to do so by means of a campaign of assassinations, by organizing a general strike, or by launching a wave of civil disobedience is not a moral question at all, but exclusively a strategic one. He is quite scornful, for instance, of those who propose limits on permissible tactics in warfare, such as prohibiting indiscriminate bombardment of civilian populations or the use of chemical weapons – constraints that he dismisses as "bourgeois."[12]

All questions about how we should resist, according to Trotsky's amoralism, should be treated as questions of political strategy, about what sorts of militancy are likely to be most effective. There is no place for moral assessment independent of the question of whether they effectively advance the ultimate aims of the movement. The idea that one might remove an effective tactic from the menu of options in a fight for a just cause, simply because of some moral constraint, is anathema to those embracing this view.

To many people, the amoralist view seems alarming. Do amoralists really think one should apply no moral constraints to political action? Yes and no. What they believe is that politics is a special domain, marked off more or less clearly from other domains, such as interpersonal relations (where moral constraints are most at home), or technology (where maximizing control of natural or artificial processes is the primary concern). According to this view, moral ideals and norms are out of place in the political domain, where the main reference points are not right and wrong, but friend and foe, and where securing victory in a struggle against adversaries is the primary consideration. According to the amoralist, morality enters the picture when one is deciding whether to engage in political action or to disengage from it. But political action itself is a domain where moral considerations are fundamentally misplaced. Once it has been decided to resolve a conflict politically, one should suspend one's moral agency and focus political strategy to maximize the prospect of prevailing over one's adversaries.

If the amoralist is correct, then the liberal is indeed mistaken. The liberal objection claims that militancy is a failing because it fails to satisfy the standard of deliberative virtue. According to the amoralist, however, this standard, like all normative standards, has no application in political activism. It is a misplaced judgment, rather than a false one: it judges with criteria that have no application to this domain. Thus, it is not that militancy is a virtue rather than a vice. It is that militancy is beyond this kind of evaluation altogether.

Is this a plausible rebuttal to the liberal objection? In my view, it is not. As an attempt to respond to the liberal, it is vulnerable to what I call the interpretive problem. The amoralist misinterprets the nature of political engagement within justice-seeking social movements. While it makes sense to depict the role of the political strategist (or indeed the military commander, a role Trotsky played as head of the Red Army) as narrowly focused on strategic calculation, it does not make sense to interpret participants in social movements generally in this way. Perhaps a union strategist, contemplating tactics that might enable a striking union to prevail against an employer, should bracket out considerations of morality. But that does not mean that union members in general ought to do so, or even that they can. They participate in the strike as workers, as members of the community, as parents, as neighbours, as co-workers. The insulation of strategic calculation from the moral assessments and constraints that regulate the rest of their lives is neither workable nor desirable. They will want to conduct the strike in a way that they can explain and justify to their neighbours, their coworkers, and so on. These conversation partners will expect the justification to be as sensitive to moral considerations as to strategic ones. It will not be enough to suggest that it doesn't matter that it was immoral, it only matters that it worked.

Moreover, social movement participants regard their participation in social movements not only as efficacious, but also as righteous. They think of themselves as doing the right thing, as partisans not only of their allies as opposed to their foes, but of justice and democracy as opposed to injustice and oppression. Amoralism, then, relies on an interpretation of political engagement that diverges both from how movement participants understand their own actions, and from how others with whom they will interact regard their actions. The insulation of resistance from the responsibility to answer normative criticisms is not sustainable.

Amoralism, therefore, makes some sense as a self-interpretation for political strategists, in their capacity as dispensers of strategic advice. But it is quite unconvincing as an excuse to exempt oneself from replying to moral objections to the use of militant tactics in social movement activism. Neither protesters nor their critics will interpret resistance as a technical domain outside the realm of normative debates.

The Consequentialist Reply

Unlike amoralism, consequentialism accepts the basic assumption that we can and should make normative judgments about the soundness of political tactics. But consequentialism denies that the appropriate standard is that of deliberative virtue. Rather, to the consequentialist, sound political action should be welfare-maximizing. In other words, one should always act so as to produce the most favourable balance of benefits over harms, taking everyone's interests equally into account. (Readers may recognize this position as the principle of utility, popularized by philosophers Jeremy Bentham and later John Stuart Mill).

In this view, whether an action is right or wrong does not depend on the nature of the act itself, but on the likely impact of performing the act under the circumstances. Should I ever lie to a friend? It depends. If my friend Tex is in a rage, thirsting for vengeance after being insulted at a bar, it would probably be for the best if I lied to him about where I last saw his hunting rifle. Under the circumstances, it would be wrong not to lie. In another case, where the anticipated consequences are different, the morality will be correspondingly different. Consider another example: Should I kill an innocent person? If, in a certain situation, killing one person would save dozens of others from being killed, then the consequentialist would regard it as wrong not to kill that one person. The right thing to do is always to act so as to maximize the goodness of anticipated outcomes, that is, the balance of benefits over harms.

The implications of this consequentialist view for an assessment of militancy are far-reaching. In an early work from 1845, Karl Marx's long-time collaborator Friedrich Engels made this well-known point:

> If one individual inflicts a bodily injury upon another which leads to the death of the person attacked we call it manslaughter; on the other hand, if the attacker knows beforehand that the blow will be fatal we call it murder. Murder has also been committed if society places hundreds of workers in such a position that they inevitably come to premature and unnatural ends. Their death is as violent as if they had been stabbed or shot. . . . Murder has been committed if thousands of workers have been deprived of the necessities of life or if they have been forced into a situation in which it is impossible for them to survive. . . . Murder has been committed if society knows perfectly well that thousands of workers cannot avoid being sacrificed so long as these conditions are allowed to continue. Murder of this sort is just as culpable as the murder committed by an individual. At first sight it does not appear to be murder at all because responsibility for the death of the victim cannot be pinned on any individual assailant. Everyone is responsible and yet no one is responsible, because it appears as if the victim has died from natural causes. If a worker dies no one places the responsibility for his death on society though some would realize that society has failed to take steps to prevent the victim from dying. But it is murder all the same.[13]

Philosopher Slavoj Žižek (who is perhaps not explicitly a consequentialist, but is in solidarity with consequentialism on these points) encapsulates this concern in a concise and vivid phrase. He calls this the problem of "systemic violence," the violence that proceeds if we do nothing, by the working of poverty and other social structures that inflict routine, institutionally organized harms on people.[14] Engels and Žižek draw a similar conclusion from these considerations. If one could put a stop to ongoing systemic violence, but one failed to do so, then one would be complicit with that systemic violence. In effect, one would participate in it by refusing to resist it, as Malcolm X would say, "by any means necessary."[15]

From the consequentialist point of view, the liberal's reluctance to intervene forcefully in order to stop systemic violence, when the opportunity exists, is unforgiveable. The liberal objection against militancy, that it is coercive and undemocratic, assumes that refusing to engage in militant resistance is somehow innocent. On the contrary, inaction often inflicts moral injuries far more grave than any that can be attributed to most militants.

Note, however, how different this view is in contrast to amoralism. The consequentialist turns the tables on the liberal, accusing nonmilitants of murder by omission, killing by refusing to rescue. As such, the consequentialist is a moralistic figure, but one who counterposes a consequentialist moral ideal (always act to maximize benefit and minimize harm) to the liberal's democratic ideal (always act so as to resolve conflict by means of reason-guided public discussion).

According to the consequentialist view, then, militancy is normatively sound as long as it maximizes net welfare. The liberal is therefore wrong to claim that confrontational protest must always be unsound. Instead, it depends on whether or not, in a particular case, it actually makes things better. Often, the consequentialist would say, it will make things better, overall, even if it imposes real costs. In those cases, at least, militancy will be a virtue.

Here we have a view that is more sophisticated than either the liberal objection or the amoralist reply. But does it succeed at rebutting the liberal's critique of militancy? Unfortunately, it does not. The problem is that, even if the consequentialist's critique of systemic violence is sound – and I believe that it is, at least to a certain degree – nevertheless, it is vulnerable to a compelling counterargument. I follow British moral philosopher and noted critic of utilitarianism Bernard Williams in calling this the integrity problem. This is a vulnerability to which consequentialist moral judgments are notoriously subject.[16]

Consequentialism demands that I act to produce the best outcome overall. But it makes no distinction between the question of what would be best to have someone do, and the different question of what it would be best for *me* to do. It assumes that these will coincide. Often, they do. But they come apart whenever what would be best overall can only be brought about by me acting in ways that are grossly at odds with my firmest commitments and core values. In cases of that kind, Williams argues, my acting so as to produce the best outcome would entail violating my very sense of who I am and why I care about what I do. I would have to set aside the roots of my moral concern, which are the values and projects that make me who I am.

It is in this sense that the problem is described as one of integrity. The consequentialist demands that I be willing to act contrary to my deepest value commitments. If I do that, however, then my actions will run counter to everything I stand for. For militant social movement activists, this is no mere technicality. It has immediately practical significance.

For example, suppose I am locked in a struggle against the banking industry, and I calculate that the way to maximize welfare is to encourage racial resentment against a stereotype of "Jewish bankers," in order to build public opposition to the financial services industry. Should I adopt this racist tactic, since I know it will help a just cause prevail, and thereby produce the best outcome? I could not, of course, because I would regard it as unthinkable, and contrary to my deeply held convictions, to use anti-Semitic stereotypes to gain a tactical advantage, even though such manoeuvres might make victory in a just cause more likely. Were my erstwhile allies to adopt this tactic, I would have to disassociate myself from them and indeed to treat them, too, as adversaries. The problem, in short, is that activists are committed not only to securing beneficial outcomes, but also to doing so in a way that they can accept as consistent with what most matters to them. Yet, to the consequentialist, this insistence on integrity violates the standard of civic virtue.

The integrity problem is fatal for the consequentialist rebuttal, not just because of a single imaginary counterexample, but because this example illustrates a deep flaw in the consequentialist conception of how to evaluate political actions. If I am to act politically, I have to be able to regard my actions as at least minimally consistent with my aims. The liberal objection highlights one of the core values of militant protesters themselves – the value of inclusive, reason-guided public discussion – and asserts that this value is contradicted by the militant's tactics. Any reply that relies on denying the value of integrity (consistency of militant action with militancy's vocation) could be seen to concede that the militant indeed acts without integrity.

The Pluralist Reply

Like consequentialism, pluralism accepts that normative judgments can be made about whether militancy is sound or unsound. Many advocates of militancy refer to pluralism as "diversity of tactics," an idea promoted by a great many people who identify with tactical militancy, at least in North America, although they may not always agree about what this phrase means.

There are two seemingly distinct ways to describe pluralism. On the one hand, there are those, like Peter Gelderloos, who emphasize the generic idea of diversity in the sense of nonuniformity: "We are advocates of a *diversity of tactics,* meaning effective combinations drawn from a full range of tactics that might lead to liberation. . . . We believe that tactics should be chosen to fit the particular situation, not drawn from a preconceived moral code."[17] Others, like prominent anarchist intellectual and activist David Graeber, emphasize the idea that tactical choices of particular individuals or groups should not be publicly criticized or regulated by other individuals or groups: "Diversity of tactics," he says, "means leaving such matters up to individual conscience, rather than imposing a code on anyone."[18]

The best way to understand pluralism is to acknowledge that it is really two distinct norms, often blended together in a manner that generates confusion. First, pluralism proposes what I call the broad spectrum rule, which prescribes that a very wide range of tactics should be considered as available in principle for use by justice-seeking social movements, including not only the use of uncontroversial tactics (notably ones deemed to be "nonviolent"), like marches and sit-ins, but also the use of more controversial tactics, like sabotage, kidnapping, or armed attacks. Obviously, one should judge each tactic's suitability to a situation on a case-by-case basis, and some forms of struggle may be inappropriate in all but the most unusual contexts, but the broad spectrum rule dictates that nothing (or almost nothing) should be taken off the table in principle.[19] Second, pluralism proposes what I call the noncondemnation rule, which states that individuals and organizations should refrain from publicly condemning the tactical choices of other participants in justice-seeking social movements, but should instead agree to disagree. Above all, the noncondemnation rule urges that no one should publicly encourage the state to unleash a repressive response against protest participants.

Putting these two norms together, then, pluralism is the view that a broad spectrum of tactics ought to be regarded as permissible in principle for use in resistance, and that the choice of which of these tactics to deploy in particular cases should be seen as an individual decision, taken by specific persons, affinity groups, or organizations, without any of them trying to dictate to others what they should or should not do tactically, or publicly criticizing their tactical choices after the fact.

Perhaps the most influential formulation of this view is given in the St. Paul Principles, a set of norms agreed upon by organizers to establish a shared understanding for participants in a protest at the Republican National Convention in Saint Paul, Minnesota, in 2008:

1. Our solidarity will be based on respect for a diversity of tactics and the plans of other groups.
2. The actions and tactics used will be organized to maintain a separation of time or space.
3. Any debates or criticisms will stay internal to the movement, avoiding any public or media denunciations of fellow activists and events.
4. We oppose any state repression of dissent, including surveillance, infiltration, disruption and violence. We agree not to assist law enforcement actions against activists and others.[20]

Only the third principle qualifies as a direct challenge to the liberal objection, which condemns militant tactics in liberal-democratic societies; a direct articulation of the noncondemnation rule, it rejects such criticisms, at least when they are made in public. In principle, though, the broad spectrum rule does not itself approve of any particular militant tactic, but simply insists that they be deemed available as options for consideration in specific cases.

However, the pluralist view arose as a response to a practical manifestation of the liberal objection: the denunciation by certain liberals of global justice protesters at the Seattle anti-WTO demonstrations in 1999 who carried out property destruction in the context of a black bloc formation. In a few cases, liberals took extreme measures to oppose these actions, either by physically assaulting bloc participants or by encouraging the police to arrest them. To the extent that pluralism represents a kind of backlash against the most sinister side effects of the liberal objection to militancy (namely, the encouragement of antiprotester violence or repression), it can be welcomed in part as a healthy corrective.[21]

But does it work as a convincing response to the liberal objection? Let's spell out the basis for pluralism more explicitly. In one early articulation (predating the St. Paul Principles by about eight years), a network of leftist groups calling itself the A16 Revolutionary Anti-Capitalist Bloc justified the noncondemnation rule in the following terms:

> We feel that the power of each group to organize autonomously based on their own ideas shows the strength of our movement. We would like to emphasize this. . . . We believe that the most effective protest is each group autonomously taking action and using the tactics that they feel works best for their situation. We do not advocate one particular tactic but believe that the greatest diversity of tactics is the most effective use of tactics. We are critical of ideologically motivated arguments that oppose this. This is why we do not believe that it is organizationally principled for any one group to set the guidelines for the protests.[22]

This passage makes plain that the noncondemnation rule assumes that there is no single normative standard for evaluating the soundness of forms of resistance. On the contrary, everyone has both a right and a responsibility to make that kind of judgment independently, using the standards that seem most appropriate to them.

This is an odd proposal. For one thing, the principle that one should not publicly criticize a tactic is self-contradictory, because publicly criticizing a tactic can itself be a tactic (designed to distance some protesters from the actions of others). Thus, in codifying the noncondemnation rule, the third St. Paul Principle implicitly violates itself by condemning those who tactically issue condemnations of the tactical choices of others.

This may seem like a philosophical technicality, and perhaps it is. However, it is odd in a more substantive way to demand of people who make sharply diverging tactical choices, rooted in competing and incompatible strategic orientations, that they should refrain from debating their differences in public. Let's imagine a major protest march is being organized, and two of the key groups planning the resistance are a large, established, staff-led NGO, and a small, more combative, grassroots antiracist organization. To the shock of many organizers, a staff member for the NGO says to a reporter that it would be helpful to have a large police presence at the demonstration. Inquiries reveal that this was not a personal view only, but reflected the NGO's deliberate choice to encourage co-operation by event organizers with the police. The grassroots organization, on the other hand, is concerned that a heavy police presence undermines the antiracist message of the march itself, and may deter broad participation in the protest because groups known to be racially targeted by the police may regard the protest as occurring on unfriendly terrain. Considering whether to publicly repudiate the statements from the NGO staff member, the antiracist organization faces a dilemma. The noncondemnation rule would close off the option of a public airing of their differences with the NGO. Yet they feel it necessary to speak out on the matter. In this context, the noncondemnation rule seems like an arbitrary and heavy-handed constraint to impose on debate within a social movement.

Perhaps, however, a more charitable interpretation of pluralism is available. If social movements practise arbitrary self-censorship in this way, a likely effect would be to block access to the critical insights and collective learning that lively debate within the movement could otherwise make possible. Maybe there is another reading of pluralism, which interprets it as something more subtle than a blunt prohibition of debate.

It may well have been concerns of this type that led the organizers of the protest against the G20 meetings in Pittsburgh in 2009 to propose a more sophisticated formulation of diversity of tactics:

> We realize that debates and honest criticisms are necessary for political clarification and growth in our movements. But we also realize that our detractors will work to divide us by inflaming and magnifying our tactical, strategic, personal and political disagreements. For the purposes of political clarity, and mutual respect, we will speak to our own political motivations and tactical choices and allow other groups and individuals to speak on their own behalf. We reject all forms of red-baiting, violence-baiting and fear-mongering; and efforts to foster unnecessary divisions among our movements.[23]

This version acknowledges an important role for debate about tactics, as one of the ways that social movement participants learn from their shared experiences of struggle. It also clarifies the underlying worry that motivates the pluralist principle: the concern that "our detractors will work to divide us by inflaming and magnifying ... disagreements." It retains the idea that one ought not to criticize in public the tactics of other protesters, though it is now framed in terms of restraint to be exercised about what topics one would be willing to address in public statements. One can say that one favours some tactics over others, as long as one refrains from offering comment about the tactics of others.

How would this more subtle version of the noncondemnation rule affect my fictional scenario? Could the grassroots antiracist group proceed to publicly repudiate the NGO's encouragement of a heavy police presence? The Pittsburgh variant of the rule would allow the group to make public statements about its own tactical preferences, for instance, a preference for not encouraging a heavy police presence at a protest march, and a public statement of the reasons for this preference. However, it would retain the prohibition of explicit criticism of the NGO's actions (or, conversely, criticism of the antiracist group's tactics coming from the NGO.) This is a compromise between the free-for-all scenario where debates are aired publicly, and the austere restriction imposed by the St. Paul Principles that precludes public debate about tactics as such. In the Pittsburgh version, debate of a certain kind can proceed, but it would be restrained by a shared unwillingness to comment directly on the merits of others' tactics. Nevertheless, the way is cleared to offer detailed explanations for one's own tactical preferences, and one's grounds for making them.

These reflections clarify what diversity of tactics – and specifically its noncondemnation rule – might mean in practical terms. But can pluralism, so understood, reply effectively to the liberal objection? The pluralist challenges the liberal's assumption (shared by the consequentialist) that there is one normative standard that can, at least most of the time, serve to distinguish sound from unsound forms of resistance. This is not amoralism, which denies that normative judgment has *any* application to resistance. It only denies that a single normative standard can be applied universally. Instead, the pluralist urges all individuals or organizations to adopt and apply their own normative standards. This comes through clearly in the preamble that the Toronto Community Mobilization Network (organizing against the G20 in 2010) added to its reproduction of the Pittsburgh Principles:

> We believe that if we are to truly build a socially just world, it will take many different tactics, much creativity and many different approaches. It is this that allows us to work together even when we disagree. We work together in solidarity and respect. This does not mean we endorse everything each of us does, or that we agree on all things. But we will listen to each other, we will discuss our differences openly and honestly, where necessary, we will agree to disagree and we will support each other when attacked. . . . We know that the way to work through these needs is to hear each other with respect, to strive to understand each other and support each other even if we do not agree.[24]

In other words, pluralism affirms the multiplicity of standards, none of which is applicable to all persons and organizations as a generalizable basis for distinguishing between sound and unsound confrontation.

My aim in this book – to mount a defence of militant protest, on the grounds that it serves the democratic ideal by enabling the unheard to gain a voice – might seem to converge with the aim of the pluralists. They, too, aim to rebut attacks on militancy and to a mount an argument for giving militancy the benefit of the doubt. However, philosophically, I believe their argument is incorrect. Pluralism addresses the interpretive problem that thwarted the amoralist reply, by admitting that militant protesters do judge themselves to be acting righteously, not just as being ruthlessly efficient in pursuit of their aims. Pluralism also addresses the integrity problem that plagues consequentialism, by encouraging activists to be true to their own convictions about which tactics resonate with their ideals and serve their chosen ends. However, it is vulnerable to a different sort of defect, which I call the accountability problem.

It is one thing to argue, as I will in later chapters, that a militant tactic, such as armed struggle or the black bloc, is often defensible in the face of public criticism and debate. But it something different, and more troubling, to argue that militant tactics of that sort do not even require a substantive defence in the face of public criticism. To argue on a pluralist basis that it is improper to even pose the question of whether a tactical choice can be justified shields political actors from accountability for their tactical choices.

Let's look at the accountability problem through another fictional scenario. An Indigenous community is attempting to stop a construction project on land that they regard as rightfully their territory, a land claim that has been in dispute for years but remains unresolved. They are using a variety of legal and political strategies to try to block the development from proceeding. Meanwhile, a group of non-Indigenous activists, motivated by a desire to act in solidarity with the Indigenous nation's struggle, decides that, due to their own societal privilege, they are better positioned than their Indigenous allies to undertake the risks of a sabotage operation. They decide to set fire to the construction machinery, opting not to consult with the Indigenous community beforehand, out of a concern that consultation might unfairly expose others to criminal liability. After the sabotage has been carried out, some members of the Indigenous community applaud it, and others regard it as interfering with their own strategy and exposing them to suspicion of having encouraged or carried out the action.

As we reflect on this scenario, many problems are apparent in the activists' approach. In particular, their failure to consult with the Indigenous community into whose struggle they had intervened is misguided, at best. But setting aside the question of whether they acted rightly, can others, notably the members of the Indigenous community, reasonably be told that the actions of the saboteurs ought not to be criticized, at least in public? More specifically, is the pluralist right to suggest that the members of that Indigenous community should concern themselves only with judging the soundness of their own tactics, but refrain from demanding that the saboteurs justify their actions in the face of Indigenous criticism? This is the heart of the accountability problem with pluralism: it entails that people do not owe a justification of their actions to others, whether these others are fellow activists, third parties affected by the action, or simply reasonable members of the public.

This rather extreme idea that activists, at least militant activists, should be granted a get-out-of-accountability-free card, is false. On the contrary, we rightly expect that activists, however revolutionary or militant they deem themselves to be, should have "a decent respect for the opinions of humankind."[25] This sort of respect for the opinions of one's contemporaries and peers, and the obligation of accountability that comes with it, is given far too little weight by pluralism.

In the end, pluralism is no more able than amoralism or consequentialism to produce a decisive rebuttal to the liberal objection. There is a need to formulate a better reply.

{ Three }

The Democratic Standard

HAVING FOUND THE AMORALIST, consequentialist, and pluralist responses to the liberal objection to be unconvincing, I want to make a fresh start and offer an original account of the civic virtue of sound militancy. Why do so many of us, including militants, regard the taking of innocent bystanders as hostages, or the poisoning of an urban centre's water supply, to be unacceptable tactics, even if they are used to advance a just cause? Conversely, why do so many people take inspiration from a community that bands together to block the eviction of a neighbour, fending off the police and defying the courts? Why are many people appalled by the use of intimidation and shaming to disrupt women's access to an abortion clinic, but willing to welcome the use of disruption and civil disobedience to block logging companies from clear cutting old-growth forests?

I believe that such questions have principled and convincing answers. But to state those answers clearly, and to defend them, it is necessary to develop a normative conception of what militancy is like when it is done well. In this chapter, I propose such a conception, which I call the democratic standard of sound militancy.

A Model Case of Sound Militancy

One way to shed light on a concept that needs clarifying is to consider a model case, and to look at other cases in terms of whether they are more or less similar to the model. For instance, to decide whether there was a "revolution" in Egypt in 2011, what criteria should be applied? One can start out by examining the key features of a model case of a revolution, such as the Revolution in France in 1789. Presumably, the Egyptian revolt will share some but not all of those features. The task then is to exercise good judgment about whether it differs from the model case in crucial ways, so that we might hesitate to consider it a revolution at all, or in only relatively minor or incidental ways, so that we can with confidence speak of an Egyptian revolution. Similarly, if we start out with a model case of sound militancy, we can generalize from that case to develop criteria of sound militancy. Then we can apply these criteria to other cases, assessing how closely they approximate this standard of soundness.

My model case of sound militancy is one that is widely accepted as legitimate: the land defence at Kanehsatà:ke in 1990. Kanehsatà:ke is a Mohawk community near the town of Oka, just west of Montreal. The incident, often referred to in mainstream media as the Oka Crisis, represents one of the most celebrated and studied outbreaks of militant protest in the Western hemisphere in recent decades. About a dozen books have been published and at least half a dozen documentary films have been made about the incident, along with countless articles, dissertations, and research symposia.[1]

One of the reasons I choose this incident is that the land defence at Kanehsatà:ke is acknowledged as admirable by both advocates of armed force and advocates of nonviolence. For instance, in their important book *Deep Green Resistance*, a work notable for its advocacy of sabotage and at least limited armed force tactics, well-known environmentalist Derrick Jensen and his co-authors, Aric McBay and Lierre Keith, single out this case as "an example worth studying."[2] Although they lament the insufficient number of non-Indigenous supporters acting in solidarity, they embrace the land defence itself as an example of the kind of action that should be emulated by others. Reflecting on the events at Kanehsatà:ke, they ask: "Why does the defense of the land always fall to the indigenous people?"[3] Another, more emphatic advocate for armed struggle (as part of a diversity of tactics), Peter Gelderloos, cites the Kanehsatà:ke case as a positive example from which anarchists (like himself) can learn a great deal about how to engage in community-based resistance.[4]

On the other end of the violence-versus-nonviolence divide, Taiaiake Alfred, himself a Mohawk from the nearby Kahnawà:ke community who was involved in some of the events, also embraces the land defence as a model of the sort of "contention" that could fuel an "Indigenous resurgence."[5] Despite his own firm preference for "nonviolent contention," he speaks warmly and without ambivalence about the "real surge of anger and pride" that enabled his Mohawk nation "to stand collectively against Quebec (and later Canada) during the summer of 1990."[6] Another prominent nonviolence advocate and author of two books on nonviolent resistance, George Lakey, makes it clear that he regards the Kanehsatà:ke events as an example of nonviolence. He writes: "Social defense may not be as widespread [as action for social transformation], but it seems to be growing in recent years. In this application, nonviolent action is not used to change, but instead to defend the status quo. . . . [For example,] at Oka near Montreal, Canada, Mohawks successfully defended their ancestral land in 1991 against the planned expansion of a golf course by the town."[7]

This case, which attracts such a broad spectrum of endorsers, defies easy compartmentalization. It was an armed action, but it was defensive. A police officer was killed during an exchange of gunfire between police and the resisters, but the Mohawks exhibited remarkable restraint and took great pains to minimize the risk of death or injury. It was a radical challenge to the Canadian state and an assertion of the sovereignty of the Mohawk Nation; but it was conducted in a way that maximized the capacity of the Mohawks to explain their grievances in a compelling way to fair-minded listeners, including non-Indigenous people across Canada who were often woefully ignorant of the issues. The grievances of the Mohawks were plainly just, and their conduct was restrained, disciplined, and rigorously sensitive to considerations of decency and fairness, without limiting or repudiating a fierce and unbending stance of militant refusal. For these reasons, it is hard to find a reasonable voice that would dare to speak against the legitimacy of their actions. I can only join in this chorus of approval.

The Land Defence at Kanehsatà:ke

The Mohawk actions[8] were taken in response to a brazenly provocative decision by a local politician named Jean Ouellette, the mayor of the town of Oka, Quebec. Ouellette spearheaded a plan to take over a parcel of land that the Mohawks had long regarded as their own territory, and to use it to expand a private golf course at Oka from nine to eighteen holes. According to the Mohawks' understanding, that land had been explicitly set aside for their use by the then governor of New France in 1717. Although the land was intended for the Mohawks, in legal terms it was held in trust by the Society of Saint-Sulpice, a Roman Catholic religious order that also resided in the area. By the nineteenth century, the Sulpician priests had come to regard themselves not only as trustees of Mohawk land, but also as the owners of private land, much to the dismay of the Mohawks.

In 1936, the Sulpician Order decided that its own dwindling numbers made its ownership of such a large plot of land unnecessary, and proceeded to sell the land to real estate speculators. Later, in 1961, the town of Oka encouraged the construction of the initial nine-hole private golf course on part of this contested land. At every step of this gradual process of dispossession, the Mohawks of Kanehsatà:ke objected that these transactions were usurping their own role as the intended beneficiaries and residents of the territory and the long-time stewards of the land in question. They repeatedly appealed to Canadian courts to stop these incursions and expropriations from proceeding, and the courts persistently rejected their arguments.

Finally, things came to a head when Mayor Ouellette announced plans to double the size of the golf course, a measure that would require further expropriations of land claimed by the Mohawks of Kanehsatà:ke, including much of the wooded area they called "the Pines," and threatening a centuries-old Mohawk cemetery within the Pines.

The Mohawks' first reaction was to organize a march through the town of Oka in protest. The march was ignored by the mayor and other supporters of the plan. The Mohawks then appealed to Quebec's minister of Native Affairs, John Ciaccia, who responded with a letter to the mayor, urging him to reverse the plan. He wrote: "These people have seen their lands disappear without having been consulted or compensated, and that, in my opinion, is unfair and unjust, especially over a golf course."[9] But this appeal, too, fell on indifferent ears. The mayor and his supporters remained intransigent.

Finally, as construction machines began preparing to proceed with the golf course expansion, the Mohawks of Kanehsatà:ke moved into action, setting up a road blockade to deny entry into the Pines by the construction workers and others associated with the project. Moreover, the Mohawks positioned armed land defenders (a term I apply to all participants in the resistance, not only those who were armed) in the area. So it was clearly a case of armed, albeit defensive resistance, asserting sovereignty over the land that they had regarded as their own for many generations. Nevertheless, the Mohawks made explicit their hope that a peaceful resolution of the standoff could be negotiated.

It did not take long for the mayor to secure a court injunction, demanding that they end the blockade. When the Quebec provincial police arrived to enforce the injunction, the Mohawks refused to stand down and allow the destruction of the Pines. After the Mohawks rejected repeated demands that they remove their blockade, the police moved in with an armed assault, firing extensive tear gas at the land defenders and attempting to end the blockade by force. Although there is dispute about who fired first, there was an exchange of gunfire between the protesters and the police, lasting about twenty-three seconds, the result of which was that one police officer was shot and later died. At this point, the police retreated, abandoning several police cars and construction vehicles, which were later used to reinforce the blockade by establishing barricades and obstacles. The police assault on Kanehsatà:ke had, for the time being at least, been repelled. A long, tense siege or standoff followed.

Over the subsequent days and weeks, other Indigenous communities took solidarity actions across the Canadian state, blockading railways and roads. Most prominently, the Mohawks of the neighbouring Kahnawà:ke community blockaded the Mercier Bridge, a crucial entry point for commuter and commercial traffic onto the island of Montreal, for about six weeks.[10]

After a time, the Quebec police were replaced by the Canadian Armed Forces. But the standoff remained unresolved for two and a half months. Eventually, judging that there was little more they could do to resolve the situation and hoping to avoid needless bloodshed, the Mohawks unilaterally declared an end to the blockade. They burned their weapons and walked away, without conceding either that they were renouncing their claim to the Pines or that they had in any way acted wrongly by defending their land from the invasion. Although they made a point of not turning themselves in, as if they had been criminals, dozens were in fact arrested during their departure. Eventually, all but a few of those charged with crimes were acquitted in Canada's court system.

The federal government of Canada proceeded to purchase the disputed land (without acknowledging that it was Mohawk land[11]), ending the development plan, and bringing the crisis phase of the dispute to an end, although the status of the land remains in dispute, as before.[12]

Some Features of the Model Case

What is it about this outbreak of militancy that makes it seem so practically sound to activists across a broad political spectrum, from armed struggle proponents to nonviolence theorists? Four key elements stand out as crucial:

1. The Mohawks had a sound grievance that they had already tried without success to resolve by means of discussion and negotiation, and they correctly judged that there was a realistic chance that a blockade might succeed where discussion had failed. Thus, the blockade was only launched in response to an urgent, compelling concern that non-

confrontational means had proven unable to address. Had they established their armed blockade without first attempting to resolve the dispute in less confrontational ways, it would strike many people as premature, indeed, as a confirmation of the liberal's worry that militancy pre-empts dialogue and consensus-building. In this case, however, nonconfrontational options, such as negotiation and legal action, had been tried and were found to be fruitless. Only confrontation could have worked, and it was plausible to suppose that it could – as subsequent events confirmed – be effective.

2. This action was led by the people most affected by the grievance, that is, it was a case of Indigenous self-activity rather than a usurpation of their agency by others claiming to act on their behalf. The members of the Kanehsatà:ke community themselves conceived and carried out the action, using their own traditional decision-making processes, and supported by virtually the whole community, including Mohawks from nearby Kahnawà:ke who had rushed to Kanehsatà:ke in response to the community's appeals for assistance. Were it a case of outsiders setting up an armed blockade on behalf of the Mohawks, not under their direction and not invited by or accountable to them, the actions would have been more difficult to justify. Such a scenario would have reproduced the very disempowerment and colonial usurpation that the Mohawks were challenging. But on the contrary, every decision about how to conduct the resistance was taken exclusively by Mohawks, using their own community standards of consensus-building and consultation.
3. The effect of the action was to empower the community to govern itself autonomously. The blockade directly transferred decision-making power concerning the land under dispute into the hands of the Kanehsatà:ke community, and removed that land from the control of the market (as a commodified piece of real estate) and the Canadian state. The effect was to democratize control over the Pines, expanding the autonomy of the Kanehsatà:ke residents over decisions affecting the fate of their culture's land base and the life of their community.

4. The land defenders acted, at every stage of the process, in ways that they could defend to reasonable people, appealing to considerations of common decency and the common good. By seeking a peaceful, negotiated resolution of the conflict, by endeavouring to minimize the risk of injury or death while insisting on the need to find a just solution, and by showing an unshakeable willingness to negotiate in good faith, even when the state failed to do so, the land defenders retained throughout the capacity to credibly claim that they, and in this instance only they, were duly sensitive to the democratic values of common decency and the common good.

Why do these four features of the Kanehsatà:ke land defence appeal so widely not just to militant protesters but to supporters of democracy and social justice across a wide swath of political currents? One core value animates this whole package of features: respect for the democratic ideal. It is this fundamental respect for democracy, for popular self-rule, that shapes the motive for the Kanehsatà:ke land defence, the conduct of the struggle, and the embrace of it by others as a model case of sound militancy. It has democratic legitimacy. To be more precise, the land defence was systematically sensitive to the core democratic value of public autonomy, or "government of the people by the people." The land defenders at Kanehsatà:ke proceeded throughout their struggle on the basis of one central implied declaration: Here, on Mohawk land, we rule ourselves.

Already, the outlines of a rebuttal to the liberal objection are coming into view. That objection's core assumption, that confrontational protest does not show due respect for the democratic ideal, manifestly fails to capture the dynamic at work in the model case.

Principles for a Democratic Standard of Soundness

The Kanehsatà:ke land defence offers a broadly accepted example of an action that is both unambiguously militant and widely admired. We can extract from this model case general principles that could be used to analyze other cases, to see where they diverge from the model case, to frame the debate about whether they diverge in ways that undercut their claim to soundness, and to help steer militancy toward admirable forms.

Taking the key features of the Kanehsatà:ke example as a guide, I formulate a set of four principles for a democratic standard of sound militancy. The standard can serve as a guide for when, and in what ways, one should set aside discussion and resort to adversarial and confrontational protest in order to apply forceful pressure, while ensuring that these actions remain faithful to the ideal of public autonomy that justifies the protest in the first place. It will also serve to rebut the liberal objection that militancy is inherently coercive and undemocratic, and thus to succeed where amoralism, pluralism, and consequentialism all failed.

Opportunity Principle

First, consider what triggered the militancy in the model case. The land defenders at Kanehsatà:ke had a serious concern, and their efforts to find a resolution, over a period of many generations, including specific efforts in the months leading up to the crisis, had proven fruitless. And yet, just as their land was about to be irreversibly expropriated by a construction project, they saw an opportunity to intervene in a more confrontational way, by blocking access to the roads that construction vehicles would have to use. If they could hold their ground in the blockade, they could stop the project from proceeding. At this point, they acted. And no reasonable person could have accused them of acting hastily or prematurely.

Noting the normative core of this approach, and generalizing from it in a principled way, I propose this as a first principle for a democratic standard of sound militancy:

> *Opportunity Principle:* Militancy should create new opportunities to resolve substantive and pressing grievances, when attempts to do so through reason-guided public discussion are thwarted by intransigent elites or unresponsive institutions.

This principle highlights three features of sound militancy: it addresses substantive and pressing grievances; it effectively creates opportunities to hasten or facilitate the resolution of those grievances; and it proceeds only when nonmilitant tactics have proven fruitless, due to obstruction by intransigent elites or unresponsive systems of power.

The first feature discourages recourse to militancy that is motivated by frivolous or trivial complaints. If, for example, a men's rights group were to block access to a subway system in order to draw attention to their "plight," well-informed people would quickly point out that (however "gender" as a system can affect everyone in adverse ways) men are systematically advantaged, not disadvantaged, by the prevailing gender system. For this reason, their grievance would be deeply questionable. A conception of sound militancy has to be able to distinguish between militancy of that kind, which is motivated by a complaint that is neither substantive nor pressing, and the militancy of exploited, oppressed, or excluded people whose confrontational resistance responds to real and important injustices.

Second, sound militancy holds out the realistic prospect of success. This point helps mark the difference between occasions when confrontational resistance can be effective and occasions when it is merely expressive or venting, or worse, when it is counterproductive or self-defeating. For example, if the use of militant confrontation would actually hinder the resolution of a serious grievance, then in that case, militancy would switch from being a challenge to injustice to being a support for it. It is quite fair to complain about militancy, and to question its soundness, if it functions objectively as a support to the problems it purports to contest. The traditional function of the *agent provocateur* is to initiate confrontation in a context when its use is deemed advantageous to the authorities, perhaps to thwart a developing alliance between resistance groups, to poison the atmosphere during delicate negotiations, or to spark an antiprotester backlash in the wider society. Critics may object to confrontational protest when its use seems self-indulgent and oblivious to considerations of strategic efficacy or predictable adverse consequences.[13] At times, the criticism may well be unfair or unfounded. But if it holds, then one should concede that such objections bear on the soundness of the militancy.

The third point, that nonconfrontational resistance should already have proven ineffective, discourages confrontational protest that is manifestly premature. Because militancy sets aside discussion with adversaries, and the democratic ideal encourages decision-making on the basis of consensus-seeking, one needs a plausible rationale for repudiating dialogue. Militancy is a civic virtue, but it is a remedial virtue: a virtue that is only admirable because it is often needed to solve a problem. The intransigence of elites and the unresponsiveness of institutions make it impossible, in many cases, to resolve disputes by means of dialogue. Because intransigence and unresponsiveness play such a key role in justifying militancy, it is usually necessary to attempt nonconfrontational resolution first, and to embark on confrontation only when the path of dialogue or negotiation is closed off. As Ann Hansen, a member of the former Vancouver-based militant organizations Direct Action and the Wimmin's Fire Brigade, points out:

> In general it is important to use . . . militant actions only as a last resort after all possible peaceful and legal measures have been exhausted, because the repercussions for everyone in the popular movement are always severe. If the popular movement does not see clearly that there is no other option left than militancy, then they may resent and blame militants for the inevitable repression from the state.[14]

In some cases, where a forceful police response is less likely, I would suggest that unresponsiveness may plausibly be assumed, once a pattern of persistent unresponsiveness or intransigence has been well established. Law professor Joel Bakan has convincingly argued, for example, that corporations are inherently incapable of overriding considerations of profit-maximization in favour of moral or ecological concerns.[15] Widespread understanding of this feature of corporate decision-making renders the process of establishing a need for confrontation less protracted than it might be in the case of an institution, such as a charity or a university, seen by many people as potentially sensitive to moral considerations.

Agency Principle

The land defenders at Kanehsatà:ke manifested a deeply democratic sensibility in the way they avoided having a small group displace or usurp the aggrieved group's capacity for agency and self-activity, by organizing themselves in a grassroots, community-based, and autonomous manner. From this, I derive a second principle:

> *Agency Principle:* Militancy should encourage the most directly affected people to take the lead in securing the resolution of their own grievances.

This principle encourages militants to resist any inclination they may have to usurp the agency of the people on whose behalf they claim to be struggling.

One of the ways that militancy can be unsound is that it can reproduce the very silencing and marginalization that it purports to oppose. If militant activists, proposing to advance the cause of immigrants and refugees, organize in a way calculated to spark street-fighting with neo-Nazis or the police, the predictable effect is to make it unlikely that recent immigrants or refugees will participate in significant numbers in these activities. The consequences of getting into legal trouble would be disproportionately harmful to them, even increasing the chance that they would be deported or denied refuge in the country. By organizing in a manner that seems almost calculated to discourage participation in the movement by people whose grievances are ostensibly central to it, a campaign of that sort shows insufficient respect for the democratic ideal; the agency principle can highlight this danger and steer militants away from it. (This is not a point about street-fighting; agency can be usurped just as easily by adopting tactics that the state encourages, such as backroom lobbying.)

Autonomy Principle

Far from empowering the institutions and elites that they opposed, the land defenders' forms of struggle shifted power over what happened in the Pines, and the fate of their claim to the land, toward the community itself, weakening the capacity of the state to unilaterally dictate to the Mohawks. In this way, their militancy was directly democratic in its effect, because it enhanced public autonomy. Generalizing from this case, I suggest a third principle:

> *Autonomy Principle:* Militancy should enhance the power of people to govern themselves through inclusive, reason-guided public discussion.

This principle addresses a concern about the relationship between militancy and the democratic ideal. Many militant resisters do not like to admit it, but some varieties of militancy, in some contexts, have the predictable effect of enhancing the capacities of a justice-seeking social movement's adversaries and weakening the strategic position of such movements.

For example, many types of militancy attempt to engage the state on terrain that is, most of the time, uniquely favourable to the state itself. The two most favourable types of terrain from the state's point of view are the legal system, where the rules are established with the state's ends in view, and contests of armed force, where the superior training, equipment, and co-ordination of the police and the military vastly advantage the state over oppositional movements. That does not mean that working through the legal system or using armed force are never sound. The land defence at Kanehsatà:ke was preceded by a legal challenge and involved the use of weapons. However, it does mean that such tactics only show due respect for the democratic ideal if they proceed in a manner that is likely to enhance the power of the public to govern itself, rather than weakening or diminishing that power.

Actions that run the risk of empowering the state, whether by offering excuses for a criminalization of protest or by shifting the terrain of struggle toward state-friendly settings, should only be pursued if there is a strategic plan for how to overcome these consequences. For example, if a law-and-order crackdown can be expected to ensue after a tactic is launched, it should not be launched without a plausible plan for defeating or repelling such a crackdown. In the absence of this kind of sensitivity to a tactic's impact, militants risk working against democracy and undermining public autonomy.

Accountability Principle

When confrontational protest is properly sensitive to the value of public autonomy, it does not shy away from controversial or unpopular actions, but it does exhibit a decent respect for the opinions of humankind, manifested in a willingness to explain its rationale in terms that others could in principle accept. From this, I derive the final principle of the democratic standard:

> *Accountability Principle:* Militancy should limit itself to acts that can be defended publicly, plausibly, and in good faith as duly sensitive to the democratic values of common decency and the common good.

This is not to be confused with only doing things that most people, or all people, agree with. But sound militancy should act only in ways that militants are willing and able to defend, in the court of public opinion, in terms that reasonable people could recognize as consistent with core democratic values.

To justify one's actions in public, within democratic politics, one has to be able to defend one's behaviour in terms of the dignity of each and the welfare of all. And to act in ways that one cannot, or would not, be willing or able to defend in these terms is to exempt oneself improperly from one of the constitutive demands of democratic politics, the demand to give an account of oneself to one's peers. Acting in this way shows scorn for the value of public autonomy.

Militancy that does not respect the opinions of humankind, in this minimal sense, should not be mistaken for sound militancy. On the contrary, it takes its cue from the elite behaviours that the public rightly regards with suspicion and contempt. Sound militancy should be willing and able to offer justifications to the broad public, to distinguish itself from the antidemocratic approach to politics of those who regard justification as unnecessary.

Rebuttal to the Liberal Objection

The democratic standard that I propose takes a different tack from the amoralist, consequentialist, and pluralist replies to the liberal objection. It assumes that, far from undermining democracy by switching from dialogue to confrontation, militancy defends and upholds the democratic ideal by making this shift. Militancy does so by weakening the capacity of elites and institutions to thwart reason-guided public discussion from dictating the terms of social co-operation. Militant confrontation is not a foe, but the best friend of reason-guided public discussion.

What initially made the liberal's concern so challenging to the militant was its basis in the very impulse that animates most militant protesters in the first place: a sense of the importance of public autonomy. The Zapatista assertion that the people rule here is at the heart of what militant resistance attempts to establish: outposts or outbreaks of public autonomy, which push back against the rule of money and power, and open up spaces for silenced or ignored publics to begin to dictate the terms of social co-operation on the basis of grassroots democratic deliberation about the public interest and the requirements of justice. Militant resistance is thus supposed to be more democratic than what it opposes, more democratic than rule by markets or bureaucracies, for instance. But the liberal challenges all this by depicting militancy as less democratic than rule by bankers, bureaucrats, or politicians.

If the liberal's depiction of militancy as antidemocratic rang true, the liberal objection would be a powerful one. But in my view, the liberal gets at least one thing right, and at least one thing wrong. The liberal is right that democracy – the self-governance of the people – is a weighty value, of overriding importance. No one's political practice can be counted as sound unless it shows due regard for the importance of public autonomy. This conviction is at the heart of the democratic standard set out above. Moreover, the liberal is also right to suppose that, at least sometimes, the way to show due regard for the importance of public autonomy is by committing to the rigours of its demand for dialogue and communicative rationality. Sometimes, that is to say, due regard for the democratic ideal is best shown by repudiating forceful pressure, among other things, and submitting to what Jürgen Habermas famously called "the unforced force of the better argument."[16]

Nevertheless, the liberal is wrong about something, too. In part, the liberal assumes that public dialogue and reason-guided discussion are self-justifying – that they are, as it were, good in themselves. But dialogue and reason-guided discussion are not equivalent to the democratic ideal, to which we ought to show due regard. They are ways of instituting the democratic ideal, social practices that derive their appeal from a commitment to the democratic ideal. The democratic ideal itself, however, is equivalent to the self-governance of the people *by means of* inclusive, reason-guided public discussion. Discussion is the instrument – the vehicle – of public autonomy, not a suitable stand-in for it.

By equating democracy not with self-governance (which uses public discussion), but with the process of public discussion itself, the liberal goes badly astray. In no small number of cases, a restriction of grievance-motivated collective action to public discussion and dialogue – which is what the liberal demands – would take effect against a backdrop of intransigent elites and unresponsive systems of power. Public officials will insist that there is no alternative; corporations will respond only to monetary incentives, ignoring pleas to respond to considerations of equity or justice.

How can due regard for the democratic ideal be shown in the face of such intransigence? Presupposing a direct equivalence between the democratic ideal and the process of reason-guided discussion, the liberal would have us simply argue with these intransigent elites and unresponsive institutions. This is at the heart of the liberal objection to militancy. If a corporation or a politician is persistently unresponsive to arguments and reason-giving, the liberal would have resisters follow up with further arguments. It is as simple, and as unconvincing, as that. Above all, the liberal would discourage setting discussion to one side and deploying forceful pressure, such as defiance, disruption, or sabotage. That, after all, would involve a cessation of the discussion, a repudiation of dialogue as the necessary form of civic engagement. But here we see that the liberal objection was wrong from the beginning. As King's depiction of a riot as the language of the unheard reminds us, the militant's recourse to forceful pressure is not a departure from the democratic ideal. It is, on the contrary, a particularly rigorous form of fidelity to that ideal. Militants, with their commitment to meet intransigent elites and unresponsive institutions with grievance-motivated, adversarial, confrontational collective action, are dialogue's only friends, under the circumstances.

At times, one can advance the democratic ideal directly, by entering into dialogue with others. At other times, however, the intransigence of elites or the unresponsiveness of systems of power renders this dialogical option unavailable. In such circumstances, the democratic ideal may best be advanced by blocking traffic to press a persistently ignored political demand; or by disrupting a business to undermine the profitability of its environmental irresponsibility; or by liberating protesters from police custody, pre-empting efforts to silence dissent through the lawless practice of arbitrary jailing, which remains so typical of protest policing.

In light of these considerations, we cannot take seriously the liberal's claim that, when militants opt for forceful pressure over dialogue, they turn their back on the democratic ideal of decision-making by means of inclusive, reason-guided public discussion. On the contrary, fixating on dialogue as an all-purpose process, to be indulged in endlessly even when elites and institutions are impervious to interventions of this kind, is itself a betrayal of the liberal's declared allegiance to the value of public autonomy. In such contexts, the liberal's ideal citizen is far less democratic than the kind of militant highlighted by the democratic standard.

At this point, the basis has been laid for Part II, in which I review several varieties of militant resistance, using the principles of the democratic standard to highlight the form they ought to take. I take the stance that all of the tactics I consider are sound some of the time, but none are sound all of the time. The way to tell the difference is to keep the notion of autonomous democracy in mind: militancy is sound when it remains loyal to the idea that people should rule themselves.

{ Part II }

Applications

{ Four }

Civil Disobedience

In practice, militant protest is almost always illegal, if only because resistance is so often criminalized as soon as the authorities begin to fear that it might prove effective. But civil disobedience puts defiance of legal authority at the centre of its activity. It violates the law not in passing, while doing something else (like causing a disruption or damaging property), but specifically by using defiance of the law to communicate with the broader public. If its practitioners found their actions to be permitted by the law, they would have to stop and do something else; the illegality is crucial to what they are trying to accomplish.

However, civil disobedience is also the least controversial form of militant protest. It is especially popular with egalitarian liberal political philosophers, like John Rawls, Ronald Dworkin, and Jürgen Habermas, who tend to be rather suspicious of other styles of militancy.[1] This is at least partly due to civil disobedience's association with a stance of strict nonviolence, which in this context means that it precludes the use of physical force. Commentators disagree about whether this style of protest must be nonviolent by definition. Nevertheless, the association is well-established because the most prominent practitioners of classical civil disobedience were two popular charismatic figures, Mohandas Gandhi and Martin Luther King, both of whom attached great moral importance to nonviolence or, as Gandhi would say, *ahimsa* (literally, nonharming).

Liberal political philosophers are also reassured by the distance that they believe separates civil disobedience from ordinary criminality or lawlessness. There is a paradox to civil disobedience: it combines open defiance of the law with an affirmation of sincere respect for it. King underlined this point as follows:

> I hope you can see the distinction I am trying to point out. In no sense do I advocate evading or defying the law [in general] as the rabid segregationist would do. This would lead to anarchy. One who breaks an unjust law must do it *openly, lovingly* ... and with a willingness to accept the penalty. I submit that an individual who breaks a law that conscience tells him is unjust, and willingly accepts the penalty by staying in jail to arouse the conscience of the community over its injustice, is in reality expressing the very highest respect for the law.[2]

This peculiar combination of defiance toward particular laws and the highest respect for law as such differentiates classical civil disobedience from other varieties of militancy.

The very thing that reassures liberals, however, may raise suspicion among radicals. Is civil disobedience perhaps a little too respectful of the law? After all, as disobedients like Gandhi and King themselves point out, the legal order often serves to institute injustice or to insulate it from challenge by protesters. Protesters, for the most part, interact with the legal system as an adversary. At least since Marx, in fact, radicals have complained that the very existence of the state is a standing affront to the autonomy of the public.[3] Can civil disobedience in effect be disempowering, ceding too much power to the authorities by fostering improper deference to the state?

In this chapter, I explore the paradox of civil disobedience – its law-respecting legal defiance – and the ethical concerns that this paradox raises.

The Salt March

Probably the most famous example of large-scale civil disobedience, India's Salt March in 1930, saw sixty to ninety thousand people jailed for defying the law. The salt tax laws, imposed on India by the British occupiers in 1882, established a British monopoly on the production of salt in India.[4] The laws denied the poorest people in India access to salt. Gandhi saw both moral and strategic reasons to target the salt tax. As a policy that imposed great hardship on the poorest Indians, solely for the benefit of foreign occupiers, the tax represented a grave and obvious injustice. And, because it was a source of indignation for millions of people, even as it provided a nontrivial revenue stream, it could be the basis for a large-scale challenge to the regime that would threaten the British both materially, by targeting revenues, and symbolically, by encouraging mass defiance.

The Salt March was launched only a few months after the Indian National Congress had declared independence – a declaration that the British occupiers rejected. This gave an added weight to the large-scale open defiance of the British regime that the march would entail.

The plan was for Gandhi to personally lead a march to the sea, where he and thousands of his followers would make salt, bypassing the claimed British monopoly, evading the salt tax, and openly defying the law that they were challenging. Gandhi and his fellow marchers embarked on March 12, 1930, travelling from his ashram near Ahmedabad to the coastal village of Dandi, over the course of about three and a half weeks. Thousands joined during the march, with hundreds of thousands, possibly millions, eventually joining the campaign of mass defiance of the salt tax laws that the march had initiated. Gandhi's plan was to march along the coast, encouraging others to join in the campaign, until the British arrested him. His intention was to put the British on the horns of a dilemma:

> For British officials, any course of action would play a role in Gandhi's drama. If they arrested the salt lawbreakers, they would create martyrs for the nationalist movement and confirm Gandhi's claims about their

> oppressive intent. If they let the salt resisters alone, they might sow doubt that they had the will to enforce their own laws in the face of Indian resistance. Either way they stood to lose something.[5]

After a few weeks of hesitation, the British decided to arrest Gandhi. But other prominent supporters took over from him, and the march went on; arrests of marchers continued on a massive scale, often accompanied by brutal police violence. In one case, "when mounted police moved up, leaders ordered protesters to lie down, and foot police dragged them off. When some resisted, the police rained down lathi [stick] blows on marchers and onlookers alike. Over a hundred were injured, many seriously, and [the Indian National] Congress claimed that some were killed."[6]

For their part, the protesters sometimes departed from the model of civil disobedience favoured by Gandhi. In one incident, when the British authorities banned a Congress-initiated local feeder march, "about 400 police and soldiers descended on its headquarters, cleared the streets, and pulled down the Congress flag. Leaders then called off the march." Not so easily deterred, "angry residents pursued the police back to their station . . . and hurled bricks, stones, and bottles, eventually chanting for the station to be torched. After about a half hour, the police opened fire," killing four protesters.[7]

Nevertheless, for the most part, the Salt March campaign complied with the norms of what we now understand as classical civil disobedience, with nonviolent legal defiance taking place on a massive scale. Between March and May of 1930, somewhere in the range of "60,000 to 90,000 Indians were arrested, while at least a hundred were killed by police, and thousands wounded."[8]

In the end, the British did not back down and repeal the tax. But they did negotiate concessions after the march, notably in the form of "the so-called Gandhi-Irwin pact, which allowed people to make salt for home use."[9] Perhaps more important, ultimately, the Salt March is considered one of the key turning points that raised the pressure on Britain, threatening its grip on power and weakening its shaky claim to legitimacy.

Several key features of civil disobedience are exemplified by the Salt

March. The disobedients defy the law or legal authorities as a means of (not just in the course of) protesting injustice; they use this act of symbolic defiance as a vehicle to communicate with the public, to appeal to their sense of justice or fairness; they do so without the use of armed force or other types of physical confrontation; and finally, they accept the legal penalties for their law-breaking, without resisting arrest or seeking to avoid punishment.

As Rawls sums it up, civil disobedience "expresses disobedience to law within the limits of fidelity to law. . . . The law is broken, but fidelity to law is expressed by the public and nonviolent nature of the act, by the willingness to accept the legal consequences of one's conduct."[10]

The Obligation to Obey the Law

With the benefit of hindsight, many observers, conservative and liberal alike, tend to express sympathy for the Salt March and for other historic instances of civil disobedience, such as Rosa Parks's refusal to move to the back of the bus. Plaques and monuments are erected to commemorate these events. But people who practise civil disobedience today are often not accorded the same deference by commentators or public officials.

At Western University in London, Ontario, in 2012, the university administration responded to a nonviolent silent vigil by banning two of the participants from university property for twelve months.[11] The two protesters, both journalists from the campus radio station, had joined with Palestinian human rights advocates as they stood quietly in protest with tape over their mouths.[12] In response to condemnation from the Canadian Civil Liberties Association, the university defended the bans on the grounds that the protesters had been "participating in a prohibited activity" because organizers had not sought prior permission for the vigil.[13] In a similar vein, when US environmental activist Tim DeChristopher in 2008 attempted to protest the sale of public lands for oil and gas exploitation by bidding on 116 plots of land in Utah, with no intention or ability to pay the $1.8 million price for the land, he was arrested for this illegal but nonviolent act of disobedience. Further, he was sentenced to two years in prison and fined ten thousand dollars, justified by the judge on the grounds that "civil disobedience" cannot "be the order of the day."[14] These punitive responses to contemporary civil disobedience stand in stark contrast to the retroactive celebration of civil disobedience practitioners from previous generations.

Why are present-day practitioners of civil disobedience typically arrested, banned, or imprisoned, instead of being praised as heroes? Is this sheer hypocrisy? Defenders of the practice of punishing people who engage in civil disobedience, such as conservative constitutional scholar Herbert Storing, argue that citizens have a moral obligation to comply with the law, even if they personally regard the law as wrong in particular respects.[15] This view has been in circulation at least since Plato's *Crito*, in which it is justified on various grounds, including the debt of gratitude that citizens owe to the state for the benefits it confers on them, notably order and security. In breaking the law and calling upon others to do so, conservative critics say, one violates the duty to comply and deems oneself to be above the law, unlike other citizens.[16]

One can only shudder, however, to imagine what laws and policies would remain in place today, starting with slavery, had legal defiance and unlawful protest more generally not been widely embraced by justice-seeking social movements over the years. The conservative's insistence on rigid legal compliance seems almost calculated to insulate injustice from effective challenge. Nevertheless, it is worth articulating a convincing and reasoned argument for a rejection of legal conformism.[17] Why, exactly, should one deny that everyone ought to obey the law, just because it is the law?

In his "Letter from a Birmingham Jail," King's most detailed articulation of the moral and political basis for his support of civil disobedience, he does not claim to have been wrongly accused. Yet he does claim to be upholding rather than violating the law. The contradiction is only apparent, because King regards the word "law" as having a dual meaning: there is human law, on the one hand, and natural law, on the other. One may sometimes need to violate human laws in order to uphold the natural law. In his letter, King cites an important and influential argument, which he derives from St. Augustine, but which originates at least as far back as Plato.[18] An unjust law, the argument goes, is not a law at all, where "law" means not only statutes but also judicial findings, court orders, lawful orders issued by police officers, and so on. According to King's conception of natural law, violating an unjust law is not, strictly speaking, contrary to law at all, because when the (human) law is unjust, or protects injustice, then it fails to meet one of the (natural law) tests of legal validity. Plato's *Laws* give an early articulation of this claim: "Enactments, so far as they are not for the common interest of the whole community, are no true laws."[19]

Civil disobedience almost always defies either laws that are themselves unjust (such as those that institute racial segregation), or laws that protect other unjust laws from being challenged (such as court injunctions banning protest marches). Violating these laws is only acting contrary to invalid laws. Therefore, the disobedient actually upholds a higher law, which King regards as natural law, or indeed, as "the law of God."

Far from the disobedients regarding themselves as above the law, according to King, it is the authorities within the legal system itself, including the legislators and the judges, sheriffs, and jailers, who are guilty of lawless behaviour. Although civil disobedience defies the de facto authority – the brute power – of the prevailing legal order, it does so in the name of the moral authority of law itself. The disobedient, at least in King's view, is defending the moral authority of natural law against a mistaken unjust law wrongly defended by the legal system.

King's account elucidates the sensibility of people who, though not predisposed to law-breaking in general, feel a conscientious impulse to defy the law as a form of protest. His appeal is to Christian theology, but more loosely interpreted, his natural law justification could also be accepted by non-Christians, as long as they have some similar rationale for appealing to a higher law. Indeed, the Salt March was organized mainly by Hindus, as well as by Muslims and others. And in the fall of 2007, several thousand Buddhist monks began a series of antigovernment marches in Burma (or as its government calls it, Myanmar), ignoring government bans on protest and police orders to disperse, to protest the rising cost of living generally and the removal of government fuel subsidies in particular.[20] These monks understood their actions very much in the way King understood his. They were violating regime laws in the name of a higher law; in Buddhist terms, the *dhamma* (a Pāli word so similar in meaning that it is sometimes translated as "natural law"). Many of these religious protesters saw themselves as upholding a higher law against the lawlessness of the authorities.

But although a range of religious traditions can accept law-breaking by protesters, a defence of civil disobedience is needed that does not rest entirely on religious conceptions of a higher, supramundane source of authority or natural law. These conceptions seem unsuitable to serve as a basis for justification among people who do not already share a common set of moral or metaphysical assumptions. So in the absence of a generally accepted way of identifying what natural law demands, or where it comes from, King's argument is not fully satisfying.

Gandhi's defence of civil disobedience relies less on a religious justification. Gandhi argues that the lawfulness of civil disobedience is rooted in the fact that compliance with the demands of law can take either of two forms. One can comply directly, by following the law, or one can comply indirectly, by disobeying but accepting the penalty it prescribes. As he puts it, "every law gives the subject an option to obey the primary sanction or the secondary, and I venture to suggest that the Satyagrahi [protester] by inviting the secondary sanction [i.e., the punishment] obeys the law."[21] Thus, according to Gandhi, one can comply with a no parking bylaw either by refraining from parking in the prohibited area, or by parking there but agreeing to pay the fine.

One may be sceptical of Gandhi's suggestion that breaking the rule but accepting the penalty is really compliance at all. However, it does seem plausible to describe it as a demonstration of respect for the law, even as the disobedient defies it. In this way, Gandhi offers an alternative, secular substitute for King's natural law defence of civil disobedience.

This Gandhian analysis of civil disobedience combines the militant's legal defiance with the conservative's respect or fidelity to the law. But this is what worries many militants. The essence of militancy as a civic virtue is to challenge injustice, and to defend public autonomy against its enemies. Can one do that while co-operating with the authorities and accepting the penalties they impose in their zeal to suppress dissent and criminalize resistance?

Civil Disobedience and Public Autonomy

The democratic standard gives us reason to take this worry seriously. The autonomy principle encourages militants to act only in ways that empower people to govern themselves through inclusive, reason-guided public discussion. But when the state drags those who stand up for justice off to jail, it exhibits the very intransigence and unresponsiveness that militants are admired for opposing. Does not the advice of King, Gandhi, and Rawls – to accept legal consequences, to co-operate with attempts by police to arrest and jail resisters – encourage the disempowerment of the public, and concede in some measure the legitimacy of the repressive actions of the state?

Let's contrast classical civil disobedience with another model of civil disobedience, namely, the almost four months of nightly street protests in Montreal organized as part of the 2012 Quebec student strike. The strike itself began as a legal or quasi-legal student mobilization, but found much of its activity criminalized when the Quebec government passed the repressive special law, Bill 78, which made nighttime demonstrations of fifty or more people illegal. In response, each evening, just before nightfall, protesters would gather for a march through Montreal's downtown, often banging pots and pans, in open defiance of the special law. At times, the police would try to make arrests, and usually they succeeded. However, at no point did the protesters act as though these repressive crackdowns, under a law that criminalized the most basic forms of democratic participation, were worthy of respect or co-operation. Quite the reverse: the police had to rely on their own brazen lawlessness and brute force to make arrests, always over angry objections and sometimes in spite of physical resistance by other protesters.[22] All the while, the illegal marchers would heap scorn and derision on the special law and on those who enforced it, by chanting slogans filled with sarcasm and contempt for the police and the regime.

This is another way that civil disobedience can proceed, condemning and resisting the use of the legal system or police powers to thwart public autonomy. And it does seem that, in this approach, the spirit of democracy – so alien to the special law used to silence the students – receives an unmistakable boost, which in turn rightly elicits admiration for the resisters. By pushing back against the state's attempt to dictate the terms of protest, and by encouraging not only defiance of the law but also scorn for those who would attempt to enforce it, the protesters showed a strong appreciation for the substance of the autonomy principle.

These evening marches in Montreal fit three of the four features of classical civil disobedience: open defiance of the law, the communicative use of that defiance to appeal to the public's sense of justice, and nonviolence in the sense of largely avoiding property destruction and completely avoiding armed force. But the student strikers generally rejected the fourth feature of the classical approach: willingness to accept legal consequences, without resisting arrest or evading punishment.

Many commentators regard the acceptance of penalties as crucial to civil disobedience. But acceptance of a penalty – rather than a prize or commendation – for marching peacefully in public to oppose a repressive and antidemocratic law can edge too close to complicity with unjust repression to be casually applauded as democratic.

Is it permissible to willingly accept legal penalties imposed by the authorities in retaliation for acts of protest that embody civic virtue? In some cases, I think it is, especially when going to jail is part of a larger movement strategy to make use of defiance to delegitimize a regime or a set of unjust laws and policies. But it is far from obligatory to accept these penalties.

The Montreal marchers show that civil disobedience can proceed without opting to show respect for the repressive state. But it would be going too far to say that their approach is superior to that of Gandhi and King. The tens of thousands of arrests of the Salt March participants made a powerful statement about the scale and resoluteness of the public's willingness to defy the legal authorities, and can fairly be described as a profoundly democratic moment in Indian history: an outbreak of defiant public autonomy. How could one not admire them? In the same way, reflecting on the Burmese monks who continued their marches despite relentless attacks from the police and the courts, it seems perverse to accuse them of excessive deference to the legal authorities. These resisters were, after all, acting in resolute and determined defiance of the authorities, often at great personal cost and risk; many of them were beaten or tortured. And their aims could fairly be described as revolutionary. Certainly, they were perceived that way by the authorities.

Arguably, therefore, the radical's worry seems unfounded as a practical matter, at least as applied to many important cases. Some of the most subversive social movements of the twentieth century made extensive use of classical civil disobedience, and it certainly had a salutary effect on promoting the cause of public autonomy. If anything, the experience of broad popular struggles imposing justice-motivated defeats on intransigent elites and unresponsive systems of power seems to embolden people to demand more autonomy. As one participant in one of King's civil disobedience campaigns put it, the "kind of power we felt was more forceful than all of their police force . . . and all of their dogs or billy clubs."[23]

Perhaps there is some feature of classical civil disobedience that protects it against the worry about public disempowerment. Both King and Gandhi underline the importance of self-respect in the practice of civil resistance, guidance that seems in part to offset a tendency to confer legitimacy on the constituted legal order. Gandhi repeatedly limits his notion of acceptable co-operation with the authorities by appealing to this notion. "A civil resister will not salute the Union Jack"; resisters will comply with a prison regulation only if it "is not contrary to self-respect"; they "will not perform any humiliating gyrations . . . and will refuse to take food insultingly served or served in unclean vessels."[24] King, too, underlines this theme, foregrounding the importance of rejecting humiliation as the moral basis for civil resistance: "We must maintain a sense of somebodiness and self-respect. . . . We must no longer allow our physical bondage to enslave our minds."[25]

I suggest one should maintain an awareness that classical civil disobedience, if done poorly, without self-respect, could cross the line into submissiveness or improper deference to illegitimate authority. Often, though, it has been done very well, indeed. At its best, it has given protesters a chance to experience what King called "the surging sense of strength of people who had dared to defy tyrants, and had discovered that tyrants could be defeated."[26]

{ **Five** }

Disruptive Direct Action

IF CIVIL DISOBEDIENCE IS a kind of defiance, much of what militants call "direct action" is better understood as a kind of disruption.[1] When protesters crowd an intersection to block the flow of traffic, establish picket lines to bar entry into a business, or use heckling and noisemakers to interrupt a politician's speech, it is likely that their aim is not to defy an authority, but to disrupt a social practice or system. Their actions violate some laws, by trespassing or causing a disturbance, but the illegality here is only a collateral effect of the primary aim, which is to impede dominant institutions from conducting their operations in the usual way.

Why would protesters do such a seemingly antisocial thing? Here, again, we have to recall the militant's vocation: to gain a hearing for the silenced or ignored, giving voice to the voiceless and defending public autonomy against the antidemocratic influence of intransigent elites and unresponsive systems of power. If protesters can bring a transportation system to a stop or force a business to shut down for the day, it will make it that much harder to ignore their grievances. Indeed, it will create a strong incentive for elites to pay attention, if only to look for a way to prevent a repeat of the costly interruption. At a certain point, disruption can threaten the systems of domination upon which elites depend for their rule, so they ignore serious disruption at their peril.

Underlying this approach to resistance is an assumption: disruptive militants assume that the elites and institutions whose domination they resist are interest-motivated. That is, their adversaries decide what to do on the basis of self-interested cost-benefit calculations. If the rich and the powerful calculate that they have more to gain by ignoring dissenters, then dissenters can expect to be ignored. If, however, a campaign of disruption tips the balance in the other direction, so that the powerful would lose more than they gain by pursuing an intransigent course, then it is likely that they will look for a way to at least partially appease the grievances that protesters bring forward. In this way, disruption serves to boost the prospects of public autonomy, by penalizing the intransigence of elites and the unresponsiveness of institutions.

The Logic of Disruption

The notion of disruption is usually simple to grasp and relatively straightforward to apply. Because of its simplicity and proven effectiveness,[2] it is very widely practised. Recently, the basic idea has been given a lucid presentation by a long-time disruption researcher and advocate, Frances Fox Piven. In her book *Challenging Authority*, Piven introduces a basic vocabulary for explaining the power wielded by elites and dominant institutions, and the capacity for exploited, oppressed, or excluded people to mobilize themselves to challenge that power effectively.

Social systems depend upon the creation and reproduction over time of what Piven calls "institutionally regulated cooperation."[3] That is, social practices and institutions rely on the participation and compliance of the people whom they exploit or dominate. Workplaces need employees to play along as co-operative and compliant participants in the workplace order, showing up for work and following instructions. Schools rely on the co-operation of students; prisons rely on the co-operation of prisoners. Hospitals rely on the co-operation of patients, libraries on patrons, public transit systems on passengers, and so on. This capacity to count on reliable and compliant co-operation is a source of great strength for these institutions and systems. However, it is also a source of great vulnerability, because these systems are dependent on co-operation that could be withdrawn. Piven underlines what she calls "the leverage inherent in interdependencies," meaning that the dominance of elites is also a kind of dependence on nonelites, and hence a vulnerability to resistance.[4] When people withdraw their co-operation from systems of interdependent power, they thereby acquire what Piven calls "disruptive power": the power to bring systems – that is, the institutions and practices upon which elites depend for their privileges – to a stop, at least for a time.

Once we understand how the logic of disruption works, we can see how broadly applicable, and how potent and subversive, its application can be. Perhaps the most obvious use of disruptive power as a style of resistance is the labour disruption or strike, in which workers refuse to work. In the most impressive kind of labour disruption, the general strike, the economies of entire cities are brought grinding to a halt, as the bus drivers stop driving buses, the letter carriers stop delivering the mail, the teachers stop teaching, the factory workers walk away from the assembly lines, and so on. The Quebec student strike of 2012 saw postsecondary students refuse to show up for classes, bringing the system to a halt for six full months, until their demand for a tuition freeze was met. In a rent strike, tenants refuse en masse to pay their rent to negligent landlords. Aristophanes's play *Lysistrata*, from the fifth century BC, depicts a satirical sex strike in which women from across Greece join together to end the Peloponnesian War by denying sex to their husbands. Real-life sex strikes have reportedly been held in at least five different countries over the past decade.[5] In every such strike, the basic logic is that of Piven's disruptive power: the interdependence inherent in systems of institutionalized co-operation is turned against those systems in order to empower the disempowered, so that their grievances can no longer be ignored.

Strikes, or disruptive withdrawals, are only one variety of disruption. Another common type may be called the disruptive convergence, in which a crowd physically overruns a space, so that it can no longer be used in the way required by some institution or system. For example, protesters might hold a sit-in in a politician's office, refusing to move, so that the office becomes unusable by the politician and their staff. They might crowd onto a highway or a commuter train track, wreaking havoc on the transportation system. They might set up a tent city encampment in a public park or public square, as was done in the Assemblies movement, thwarting one use of public space in order to institute a new, more challenging use. In each case, the convergence of people into a space that depends upon them moving along in the usual way makes the space unusable by a system or institution that depends upon it.

A third variety of disruption is the disruptive outburst. These occur when protesters come together to make noise or create confusion, in a manner that renders certain systems or practices unable to function. If a city council meeting is underway, and a crowd of several dozen begins to shout and chant or use noisemakers and whistles, it will bring the meeting to a stop or at least create a long delay. Disruptive outbursts can also take the form of insurgent street theatre performances in unauthorized spaces, or the Indigenous Round Dances in city streets or shopping malls held during the Idle No More upsurge of Indigenous mobilization in the Canadian state in 2012–13.[6]

Such disruptions work, then, by rebalancing incentives, making it more burdensome for elites or systems to continue ignoring a grievance, and therefore endure further disruptions, than to at least partially address the grievance.

Disruption in Action

To further explore the significance of this mode of militancy, let's consider a few examples illustrating the three varieties of disruption described above: the sit-down strikes in Flint, Michigan, and elsewhere in the 1930s and 40s; the occupation of Alcatraz island by the Indians of All Tribes in 1969–71; and the disruption of the 1968 Miss America Pageant.

The Sit-Down Strikes of the 1930s and 40s

The idea of the sit-down strike, developed by industrial workers in the 1930s, could not be any simpler. Workers would just sit down and refuse to work. But its very simplicity made it exceptionally potent. The strikes of today, when they occur at all, are constrained by narrow labour relations law and domesticated by the all-encompassing role of labour union officials as mediators between boss and worker. But a sit-down strike in the 1930s or 40s was very different. It could be launched spontaneously, in response to an immediate concern or grievance, and it would immediately begin to take its toll on the employer. After an end to the sit-down was negotiated, the workers could repeat the same tactic days later, should the employer's promises not be kept.

According to US labour historian Jeremy Brecher, the tactic of the sit-down strike was developed in Akron, Ohio, in 1933, and over the next few years became a tradition in that city.[7] But it soon spread to other cities, as well. "The sit-down idea spread so rapidly because it dramatized a simple, powerful fact: that no social institution can run without the cooperation of those whose activity makes it up."[8] The most dramatic application of the sit-down tactic happened in Flint, Michigan, in a strike against General Motors in 1946. Rather than leaving the workplace and picketing outside, the workers followed the sit-down method pioneered in Akron, and so maintained their control of the workplace, ensuring that no scab replacement workers could enter and that no machines or materials could leave the factory.

When the employers called in the police to drive the workers out, the workers and their families fought back. "After battles began with the police, women established a Women's Emergency Brigade of 350 members, organized on military lines, ready to battle police. 'We will form a line around the men, and if the police want to fire then they'll just have to fire into us,' announced Genora Johnson, one of the founders of the brigade." The Flint strike soon spread to other cities and towns. "GM's projected production for January of 240,000 cars and trucks was cut to 60,000. In the first ten days of February, it produced only 151 cars in the entire country."[9] The strike produced important victories, and the successful tactic was soon emulated by others.

> Sitdowns were particularly widespread among store employees, so easily replaced [by scabs] in ordinary strikes. Women sat down in two Woolworth stores in New York. . . . Similar sitdowns occurred in five F.&W. Grant stores; in one, strikers staged an impromptu St. Patrick's Day celebration and a mock marriage to pass the time. Having no chairs to sit down on, 150 salesgirls and 25 stockboys in Pittsburgh staged a "folded-arms strike" in four C.G. Murphy five-and-ten stores for shorter hours and a raise.[10]

One unique feature of the sit-down style of labour disruption is that it directly empowers workers themselves. It thus weakens the grip not only of employers, but also of union officials, whose control over the conduct of the strike is limited. For this reason, the desire of employers and the state to crush the sit-down tactic once and for all was given a boost by the willingness of the official union leadership apparatuses to let the tactic disappear. But, as a testimony to the potency of the disruptive-withdrawal style of militancy, the sit-down remains unsurpassed in the history of class conflict in North America.

The Occupation of Alcatraz Island, 1969–71

The second type of disruptive direct action is the disruptive convergence, typified by sit-ins and occupations of contested spaces. The occupation, or as one might also call it, the reclamation of Alcatraz Island, California, in 1969 was conceived and carried out by a group of Indigenous people in the Bay Area formed for the purpose, calling themselves Indians of All Tribes. The group's name reflected the diversity of the participants. "This protest involved people from many Indian nations," wrote Adam Fortunate Eagle, one of the organizers. "Tlingit, Iroquois, Blackfoot, Chippewa, Navajo, and virtually every other Native American tribe was represented among the thousands of Indians in the Bay Area."[11]

The 1969 reclamation was not the first one attempted by Indigenous people. Five years earlier, in 1964, "a year after the [Alcatraz] prison closed, a handful of Sioux landed on the island and staked out claims under a 100-year old treaty permitting non-reservation Indians to claim land the government had once taken for forts and other uses and had later abandoned."[12] They were expelled from the island after four hours. The federal government planned to turn Alcatraz Island into a national park, and was not interested in redressing historic and ongoing injustices. Nevertheless, the boldness of the action was not forgotten by members of the local Indigenous community.

When, in October 1969, the San Francisco Indian Center burned to the ground, "Indian people throughout the Bay Area mourned it like a close and beloved friend. Everyone asked, 'What now? Where do we go?' . . . Alcatraz immediately came to mind."[13] As members of the community met, the plan began to take shape. They would reclaim the island the next month, in November, as a reassertion of the claim made and dismissed in 1964, but also in order to found a new community centre. Beyond the crucial function of offering a meeting place for the community to assemble, the new outpost of Indigenous culture and autonomy would serve a range of functions. It would house a Center for Native American Studies, an American Indian Spiritual Center, an Indian Center of Ecology, a Great Indian Training School, and an American Indian Museum.[14] In one example of the biting irony that infused the project's initial declaration, it was announced that a small portion of the land on Alcatraz Island would be set aside for Settlers to use, with that land "to be held in trust by the American Indian Government – for as long as the sun shall rise and the rivers go down to the sea – to be administered by the Bureau of Caucasian Affairs (BCA). . . . We will offer them our religion, our education, our life-ways, in order to help them achieve our level of civilization and thus raise them and all their white brothers up from their savage and unhappy state."[15]

As the reclamation action got underway, the US Coast Guard tried to intercept the boats carrying the activists to the island. Some were stopped, but persistence and patience paid off, and the island was soon successfully reclaimed. Immediately, activists began to establish the necessary infrastructure for an autonomous community: a nursery school for young children, a system of food acquisition and preparation, a volunteer-run medical clinic, a sanitation system, and so on.[16]

They also established a system of democratic decision-making, in which every Indigenous person who had been on the island for at least a week could participate. After a year and a half of sustained reclamation, the government finally cracked down on the protest and forcibly removed the "occupiers." They did not get to keep the island, but the Indians of All Tribes could claim real achievements, most notably the electrifying impact their action had in stimulating the growth of the emerging Indigenous Liberation or Red Power movement:

> News of the occupation swept through Indian communities; our continued resistance inspired wonder and pride. After decades of indignity and soul-sickening powerlessness beyond the understanding of any non-Indian, a group of Indians had seized an island in full view of millions and held it for nineteen months despite government efforts to destroy them. Everywhere, American Indians rejoiced.[17]

It was no surprise when others took Alcatraz as a model that could be replicated. Red Power activism increasingly took the form of disruptive convergences: "A number of protest camps were established during the early 1970s, including those at Mount Rushmore and the Badlands National Monument. During the same years, government buildings also became the sites of protests," and approximately seventy-four reclamations were organized in the months during and immediately after the Alcatraz action.[18] In the end, the government's Alcatraz National Park scheme went ahead, as planned, but the cost that the government paid – first, in the boost to resistance movements, and later, in the policy concessions it had to make – was high.

The Miss America Pageant Protest, 1968

The disruptive outburst is illustrated by the Miss America protest of 1968. Long despised by feminists as a symbol of the objectification and degradation of women, the pageant looked to some activists at the time to be an ideal target for a disruptive protest. The event was to be held in Atlantic City, New Jersey, that year, and a recently formed feminist organization in nearby New York City was determined to make a forceful intervention. Their organization, New York Radical Women, included many prominent figures in the Women's Liberation movement, including Robin Morgan, Shulamith Firestone, and Carol Hanisch. In a public statement issued two weeks before the event, the group detailed their objections to the pageant and outlined some of their plans. The Miss America Pageant, they argued, was sexist (because it objectified women), racist (because of its racialized beauty ideals), and militaristic (because the winner's duties included "supporting the troops").

One of the first things organizers did was produce a leaflet advertising the event. The planned action was described, using the language of the time, in the following way:

> There will be: Picket Lines; Guerrilla Theater; Leafleting . . . ; a huge Freedom Trash Can (into which we will throw bras, girdles, curlers, false eyelashes, wigs, and representative issues of *Cosmopolitan, Ladies' Home Journal, Family Circle,* etc. . . .). . . . Lots of other surprises are being planned (come and add your own!) but we do not plan heavy disruptive tactics and so do not expect a bad police scene. It should be a groovy day on the Boardwalk in the sun with our sisters. In case of arrests, however, we plan to reject all male authority and demand to be busted by policewomen only.[19]

In an article written shortly after the protest, Hanisch explained that many organizers opposed the proposal to stage a disruption during the event itself, but when some indicated that they would proceed with or without approval, the group as a whole endorsed the idea.[20]

The protest unfolded in three segments. First, there was the main outdoor picket line and guerrilla theatre action, which was the only part addressed in the statement (hence, "we do not plan heavy disruptive tactics and so do not expect a bad police scene"). A few hundred women participated in that event, and none were arrested. Second, after a smaller group of women entered the building posing as audience members, there was an initial disruption on live television, which consisted of a banner drop, in which a large banner bearing the words "women's liberation" was unfurled from a balcony. Finally, in the last phase of the protest, two smoke bombs were released inside the seating area, interrupting the pageant and forcing an evacuation of the entire audience. Sixteen women participated in the disruption, and five were arrested.[21] "Millions of viewers saw the action and the show was stopped for ten minutes" before order was restored and the live broadcast could resume.[22]

This example, too, illustrates the logic elucidated by Piven: the unobtrusive compliance of a group of people, upon which systems of domination and exclusion had long relied, was interrupted by a disruptive outbreak of public autonomy. The effect was to tilt the balance of power in the other direction, establishing a cost to be paid by ignoring the group's grievances and aspirations, and thus establishing a new incentive to pay attention.

Democracy or Blackmail?

As these examples illustrate, the logic of disruption can be a potent force for public empowerment and a true language of the unheard. But to what extent should we think of this empowerment as democratic? There are those who paint a more ambiguous picture of what is happening in cases like the ones considered above.

At the time of his death in 2013, Ronald Dworkin was arguably the most influential voice within liberal political philosophy and legal thought. He embraced at least some kinds of civil disobedience, but he spoke for many liberals when he described incentive-based disruption in more critical terms. In his view, disruptions smack of blackmail:

> Someone who hopes not to persuade the majority to his point of view by forcing it to attend to his arguments, but rather to make it pay so heavily for its policy that it will give way without having been convinced, must appeal to some form of elitism or paternalism to justify what he does. And any appeal of *that* form does seem to strike at the roots of the principle of majority rule, to attack its foundations rather than simply to call for an elaboration or qualification of it. If that principle [of majoritarianism] means anything, it means that the majority

> rather than some minority must in the end have the power to decide what is in their common interest.[23]

Democracy, Dworkin suggests, implies a certain degree of deference by numerical minorities to majorities, and this majoritarian deference is embodied (albeit imperfectly) in electoral systems. Democratic protest, according to this view, consists of the attempt by minorities to make their case to the majority, in order to bring about remedies for their grievances. If they win the argument with a majority of their fellow citizens, they should get their way. However, as long as their preferences cannot command majority support, as represented in elected legislatures, they have a civic duty to defer to the majority's will. Meanwhile, they can continue their campaigns of rational persuasion. But there must be no attempt to coerce the majority into complying with the minority preference. Using the power of disruption to pressure the majority into acting contrary to its own preferences and judgments, out of fear of further disruption, does not make things more democratic, but less so. In effect, disruptive militancy is a form of blackmail, in which the minority rules over the majority by means of a threat.

This argument – that in disruption a minority coerces the majority in an undemocratic way – looks like a restatement of the liberal objection. My general reply to the liberal objection is that, to the extent that militancy adheres to the spirit of the four principles of the democratic standard, militant action can plausibly claim to be both committed to the democratic ideal of popular self-rule through reason-guided public discussion, and equally committed to setting aside dialogue with adversaries in order to bring forceful pressure to bear in attempting to break the intransigence of elites and institutions. What Dworkin adds is a kind of counterargument, in the form of a new insistence on the relevance of majority rule. He claims that disruption does not empower the numerical majority, but the minority, and in this way hurts the cause of democratic self-governance. In other words, disruption is a way for numerical minorities to function as counterelites who impose on the majority policies and practices that the minority cannot persuade them to embrace via discussion.

The blackmail objection is right to say that majoritarianism is a part of our understanding of democracy. But I have already argued[24] – and here I believe most contemporary liberal deliberative democrats would agree – that the core of democracy does not consist of preference-counting. Instead, it consists of decision-making by means of inclusive processes of reason-guided public discussion. The question to be addressed here is: What does one do when the intransigence of elites, or the unresponsiveness of systems of power, stands in the way of such decision-making? Should one simply accept this as the best that can be done?

Certainly not. To do so would indicate a too weak attachment to the democratic ideal of public autonomy. Something has to be done to overcome these barriers to public autonomy. In characterizing disruptive direct action as blackmail, I believe that Dworkin has mistaken democratic procedures for the substance of democracy, when in fact the substance of democracy is public autonomy.

To make the point more vivid, consider how blackmail can indeed figure in democratic politics, or ostensibly democratic politics (where voting does occur, but public self-rule may not). Suppose ten roommates are deciding whether to order pizza or Chinese food for dinner, a debate that recurs every Friday evening. One of the roommates, a man known for his stubbornness in such matters, pulls out a gun and says, "I'll kill you all, unless you vote for pizza." The vote is held, and the decision is unanimous. Everyone opts for pizza. This is a majoritarian decision procedure, to be sure. But is it democratic? After all, the ten people were choosers, whose choices were accurately tallied up. This charade of self-rule can be immediately seen through; they were not self-governing, because they acted under a threat by a minority of one, who happened to have a stark power advantage.

Dworkin regards the militant protesters, with their general strikes and sit-ins, as akin to the gun-toting pizza lover. But to see where protesters fit in, we have to make the picture more complicated. Imagine that, shortly after the vote is held, one of the others tackles the pizza lover and disarms him, while an accomplice cancels the pizza delivery and proceeds to order Chinese food, just before closing time. In this scenario, who is the blackmailer? Is it the gun-toting pizza lover, or is it the two interveners who thwarted implementation of the unanimous decision? To me, at least, it seems clear that the interveners, though a minority, and though lacking confirmation that their preference was shared by most of the others, acted in defence of public autonomy by their bold and decisive actions. We can imagine them going astray, deciding that the others were not to be trusted, and using the pizza lover's gun to set themselves up as the only ones who could decide on what to order for the next meal. In that case, they would be rightly denounced as a new elite. They would have become what they had initially opposed. But there is every reason to hope that they were acting on behalf of the public autonomy ideal, and that the larger group will emerge from the struggle with a newfound prospect of enhancing their capacity to make such decisions in a genuinely democratic, autonomous way. By disarming an intransigent bully who claimed that there was no alternative but to adopt his preference, the two interveners acted in keeping with the autonomy principle. Next time, one hopes, the decision can be made without the need for a remedial intervention of this kind.

This little parable has an obvious relevance for the militant's reply to the blackmail objection. What Dworkin overlooks is that the status quo is already a standing system of blackmail. Cut corporate taxes, or thousands will lose their jobs! Ease the stringency of environmental regulation, or production facilities will move to another jurisdiction! Apply for this low-paying, alienating job, or remain unemployed and impoverished! The power asymmetries that form the context in which ostensibly democratic elections are held call into question Dworkin's easy equation of election outcomes with the will of the people. Publics expressing support for a corporate agenda, against the backdrop of a threat that the power of big business can be used to penalize noncompliance by disinvestment, are in the same position that the roommates are in when asked whether to vote for pizza or Chinese food. They can reject the demands of the powerful, but the cost of doing so may be prohibitively high. For the decision to be a fair indication of their considered preferences, therefore, the power asymmetry would first have to be made less one-sided. Only then could we begin to think of the decision-making process as at least in part an expression of public autonomy. This is what leads militant resisters to have recourse to the logic of disruption. They intervene to offset or overturn stark asymmetries of power.

Dworkin is not wrong to worry about blackmail. In raising the issue, he underlines a norm built into the autonomy principle of the democratic standard: Militancy should enhance the power of people to govern themselves through inclusive, reason-guided public discussion. Blackmail is indeed a barrier to public autonomy, but Dworkin has mistaken the solution for the problem. If majority rule is to be secured, one cannot tolerate uncontested asymmetries of power that leave persistently and brazenly intransigent elites in such advantageous circumstances that they can silence or ignore the grievances of others indefinitely. The blackmail has to stop, so that the majority can take its place in public decision-making, currently usurped by markets, bureaucracies, and other unresponsive systems of power. The autonomy principle demands nothing less, which is what makes disruptive militancy so important for the fate of the democratic ideal in real-world public decision-making.

{ Six }

Sabotage

"TO INCITE THE CITIZEN to the active practice of simple sabotage and to keep him practicing that sabotage over sustained periods is a special problem." Ideally, though, if all goes well, "the citizen-saboteur acquires a sense of responsibility and begins to educate others in simple sabotage."[1] So says a training manual on effective sabotage tactics, prepared by the US government in 1944.

Needless to say, the idea was to encourage citizens of *other* countries to engage in sabotage, when those countries were ruled or occupied by adversaries of the US government. Still, this document makes it plain that the authorities were, at least at that time, willing to concede that sometimes sabotage is a kind of civic duty, something that the best people, the people with "a sense of responsibility," both carry out on their own and encourage others to carry out in turn.

Consider some of the techniques proposed in this document:

- "Cut telephone and telegraph transmission lines. Damage insulation on power lines to cause interference."[2]
- "Slash or puncture tires of unguarded vehicles. Put a nail inside a match box or other small box, and set it vertically in front of the back tire of a stationary car; when the car starts off, the nail will go neatly through the tire."[3]
- "Fires can be started wherever there is an accumulation of inflammable material. Warehouses are obviously the most promising target, but incendiary sabotage need not be confined to them alone."[4]

The list of suggestions is too long to reproduce, but these examples convey the general flavour of the recommendations.

To ethically sensitive people, the mere fact that the former Office of Strategic Services (now known as the CIA) promoted a particular form of political action might sow doubt about its moral or political defensibility. One rightly feels reluctant to set one's moral compass by emulating the US "security" establishment, long known for its indifference to moral considerations. But did they perhaps have a point? Perhaps there are cases where inflicting tactical property damage is the responsible thing to do, for today's citizen-saboteurs.

Monkeywrenching – The Logic of Sabotage

Sabotage has been practised for thousands of years, wherever people have found themselves forced, by the explicit threat of violence or the looming prospect of hunger, to toil on behalf of the rich and the powerful. Perhaps the most widely cited form of tactical sabotage was practised by participants in the Luddite movement of early nineteenth-century England, in which workers used mechanical sabotage to resist de-skilling, speedups, and what we now call downsizing in the textile industry. Although over the years elites have carefully cultivated a perception that this use of sabotage was a fruitless and doomed attempt to cling to the past, the fact that a military force of no less than twelve thousand soldiers had to be deployed to suppress the Luddites shows the potential potency of broadly applied sabotage tactics.[5]

Luddism was neither the first nor the last example of tactical sabotage. In the biblical Book of Judges, the story is told of Abimelech's defeat of the city of Shechem, after which he "sowed with salt" the city's farmland, to prevent the town's repopulation.[6] Later in the same Book of Judges, the sabotage motif returns. Samson ties torches to the tails of three hundred foxes and disperses them among the grain and olive crops of the Philistines, just before the harvest, burning the crops to the ground.[7] Both Abimelech and Samson typify the saboteur's preference for acting "against a specific critical target such as an essential production facility."[8]

Sabotage appeals to some activists because it offers its practitioners a tempting strategic shortcut. For example, two or three people may seem powerless to stop a so-called development project undertaken by a large corporation and supported by all the resources of the state. But if they can find a way to destroy a crucial bridge or an expensive and difficult-to-replace piece of drilling equipment, long and costly delays can be imposed on the company. This, in turn, can at least stall for time, so that more-conventional mobilizing strategies can be given a chance to work. In the most favourable scenario, it can impose prohibitively high costs on the company and encourage it to pull out of the project altogether.

In this way, sabotage – or what one of its leading advocates, Dave Foreman, prefers to call "monkeywrenching" – replicates the basic logic of disruption, examined in the previous chapter. The difference is that, in sabotage, the cost-raising impact is produced not by disrupting an institution or social structure, but by destroying a piece of equipment or infrastructure on which the adversary relies in some crucial way. The use of tactical destruction appealed to the Office of Strategic Services in 1944 for the same reason it appeals to groups like Earth First! or the Animal Liberation Front today. Sabotage can be carried out quite efficiently by very small numbers of saboteurs, acting with little or no direction or co-ordination, and with a substantial prospect of successfully evading detection and prosecution.

All that sabotage requires in order to succeed is the capacity to destroy something upon which one's adversary crucially relies. If the adversary needs to drive trucks across a river, one can take out the only bridge; if the adversary needs heavy construction machinery, one can immobilize some crucial piece of equipment.

Perhaps it is unnecessary to mention the obvious fact that destruction differs from defiance and disruption in that it involves wrecking things. I point it out, however, because some people seem uniquely troubled by this, counselling respect for property and complaining that acts of destruction seem immature, even nihilistic.

I do not regard these complaints as baseless. At times, notably when its contribution to social movement objectives remains opaque, the destruction of property may well appear immature, nihilistic, or both, even to broadly sympathetic observers and bystanders. But the problem in such cases is not the ensuing brokenness of objects. It is the failure of the destruction to have a discernible point, or the unwillingness of the saboteurs to communicate the point clearly.

Indeed, it seems doubtful that anyone regards property damage, in and of itself, as necessarily nihilistic or immature. A firefighter, wielding an axe, may destroy a door or a window in order to extract endangered people from a burning building. No one calls the firefighter immature or nihilistic, no matter how many doors she destroys in this way. We acknowledge the urgency of her objective, we understand how her destructive act contributes to achieving that objective, and we see that no less-destructive approach would have been as effective as the one chosen by the firefighter. It seems to me that the same standard applies to destruction generally, including tactical destruction by saboteurs. One can encourage the destruction when one grasps the urgency of its objective, the directness of the act's contribution to attaining that objective, and the absence of ways of achieving the same result with less destruction.

If these elements are in place, it is hard to imagine widespread condemnation of mere property destruction. At any rate, such condemnation would be unreasonable. In the absence of these elements, however, even if one shares the saboteurs' aims, one would likely disapprove of their methods. To be sure, there are those who celebrate destruction as an end in itself, regarding it as a kind of rebellion in its own right (rather than a tactic that, in some specific contexts, might be used for rebellion). But most of us can agree that destruction for its own sake is, if not nihilistic, probably immature; and if not immature, certainly indicative of a simplistic view of rebellion.

By contrast, the so-called citizen-saboteur is, in principle, replicating the form of intervention exemplified by the firefighter: using destruction, when nothing else will work comparably well, to address an urgent, pressing need. This, at any rate, is how the saboteurs normally view their own actions. Far from nihilistic or indifferent, they resort to breaking things out of the very "sense of responsibility" that the US government had tried to encourage among the citizen-saboteurs it trained.

If one admits that the firefighter may act rightly in damaging property to rescue people in danger, one can no longer justify crossing tactical property destruction entirely off the list of *potentially* justified actions. But it remains to be determined exactly when and on what basis it can be justified. In this book, I apply the democratic standard to sort out such questions. In the case of sabotage, the most important principle is that of accountability. The accountability principle encourages militant actions to be conducted only in ways that can be defended publicly, plausibly, and in good faith as being sufficiently sensitive to the democratic values of common decency and the common good.

I turn now to three typical examples to see whether sabotage can be said to meet this standard of soundness: tree-spiking by Earth First! in the US Pacific Northwest, arson attacks by Red Zora in West Germany, and some recent cases of machine-wrecking and road sabotage by ecologically motivated saboteurs.

Tree-Spiking

Tree-spiking has been one of the most controversial tactics of militant environmentalism. It was popularized by Earth First! activists in the 1980s, notably through the writing of Dave Foreman, one of the group's founders. The aim of tree-spiking is to protect forests from logging by making the trees unusable by the timber industry. Here's the description offered in the tactical handbook *Recipes for Disaster: An Anarchist Cookbook*:

> You can hinder logging in the last of our forests by spiking trees in woods that are to be cut. Using a big hammer, drive a nail at least six inches long into each trunk, above the level of your head, and cut off the heads of the nails or cover them with bark; repeat this process randomly throughout the woods, working in the rain if necessary to muffle the noise and using ceramic spikes if you need to outwit loggers with metal detectors. Inform the forest service that the trees have been spiked.[9]

The use of tree-spiking had a twofold effect on Earth First! On the one hand, it raised the profile of the group considerably, attracting attention from both the mainstream media and the police, including the FBI, once spiking was made a federal crime in 1988.[10] On the other hand, it provoked a deep rift inside the group. One current within the group saw the tactic as an effective way to remove the profit motive driving the clear-cutting that they were attempting to stop, and a second current viewed the tactic as politically self-defeating and antithetical to the strategic objective of forging an alliance with forestry workers against the timber industry corporations.

The leading voice for the pro-spiking current was Foreman, whose book *EcoDefense* made the case for tree-spiking, along with other types of sabotage:

> The value of spiking is as a long-term deterrent. If enough trees in roadless areas are spiked, eventually the corporate thugs in the timber company boardrooms, along with their corrupt lackeys who wear the uniform of the Forest Service, will realize that timber sales in our few remaining wild areas will be prohibitively expensive. And since profits are the goal, they will begin to think twice before violating the wilderness.[11]

It sounds plausible. And indeed, if it were possible to make clear-cutting old-growth forests unprofitable by spiking trees, then presumably the tactic would at least be strategically effective, if perhaps still ethically controversial.

But the leading voice of opposition to spiking within Earth First!, Judi Bari, argued that, however plausible it sounded on paper, both in practice and in principle Foreman's spiking project was bound to fail.

> There are several flaws in this theory. The strategy of tree-spiking was designed for federal lands, where most remaining old-growth in the US is located. In these cases, it is the Forest Service, not the timber company, which bears the cost, both of removing the spikes and of charging lower rates for the timber to make up for the risk of broken saws. The Forest Service is not required to make a profit, since it is financed

> by tax money. . . . There aren't enough tree spikes in the world to make a dent in this agency.[12]

Bari goes on to make a strong case against the strategic argument for spiking. I find her argument convincing on that score. But in the present context, I am more interested in the ethical debate. Strategy aside, is spiking defensible as a way of using property destruction to give a voice to the voiceless? Supposing we thought it would work, would spiking be admirable, as a language of the unheard?

Tree-spiking is designed to break saws. Given the nature of the saws used in the industry, the breaking of saws by spikes poses a risk to the physical safety of workers. Spiking advocates, like Foreman, assume that it can be done in ways that minimize risks to workers. And besides some near misses, only one worker is known to have been injured by the practice (not necessarily by anyone associated with Earth First!). A forestry worker, George Alexander, was very seriously injured by a broken saw caused by a spiked tree in 1987.

> A 12-foot section of the huge sawblade had broken off and hit George in the throat and face, ripping through his face mask and cutting into his jugular vein. His jaw was broken in five places and a dozen teeth were knocked out. The blade was wrapped around him, and his co-workers had to blowtorch it off while they tried to keep him from bleeding to death.[13]

Foreman was undeterred, responding: "I think it's unfortunate that somebody got hurt, but you know I quite honestly am more concerned about old-growth forests, spotted owls and wolverines and salmon – and nobody is forcing people to cut those trees."[14]

This is only one case, and the existence of a single serious injury caused by tree-spiking may be consistent with Foreman's view that spiking can be done safely, on the whole. However, it is hard not to think that the nature of tree-spiking, which tries to damage a dangerous saw while it is being used by timber industry workers, in effect uses these workers as instruments for targeting the companies that employ them. This may (as Foreman claims) or may not (as Bari claims) be an effective tactic, but

I find it difficult to believe that one could in good faith defend it as sufficiently sensitive to the value of common decency. Deliberately exposing one person to danger, in order to target an institution that is not controlled by the endangered person, instrumentalizes the worker in a rather callous way. Foreman's retreat from justification into self-expression ("I am more concerned about old-growth forests . . . ") and rationalization ("nobody is forcing people to cut those trees") is symptomatic of the gap between his spiking strategy and the concern to justify his tactics in reason-guided public discussion. While the concept of innocent bystanders may be vague at the edges, there can be no doubt that the workers here would normally be regarded as bystanders to the conflict between antilogging groups and timber industry firms. Endangering bystanders in this way is probably a bad strategy, but it is surely an indication that spiking advocates are insufficiently sensitive to the importance of being accountable to the public, and its standards of common decency, for their tactical choices.

The implication is clear. The democratic standard encourages activists to steer clear of tree-spiking, not out of respect for property, but out of respect for accountability: militancy must be practised in ways that can be defended publicly, plausibly, and in good faith, as duly sensitive to the democratic values of common decency and the common good. The instrumentalization of workers like Alexander flagrantly flouts common decency. It treats him as an expendable means to be sacrificed in a struggle that is not against him, but against his employer. In addition to the moral reason to treat people like him with decency, there is a strategic one as well: as Bari argued, forestry workers should be seen as potential allies in the struggle against timber firms and their enablers in government.

Arson Attacks

The use of arson as a means of sabotage is to be distinguished from what one might (borrowing military jargon) call antipersonnel arson attacks, that is, arson aiming to kill or injure people. Most of the people who use arson in the context of militant protest do not intend to kill or injure people. Rather, they typically intend to damage or destroy buildings. (I take up attempts to kill or injure people later, in the chapter on armed struggle.)

Like other types of sabotage, most recent uses of arson (at least in North America) have been broadly environmental in motivation.[15] In particular, some high-profile uses of arson have set out to damage or destroy laboratory facilities that carry out research using animals. However, I will take up a different example: the arson attacks by the feminist organization Red Zora, which operated in (West) Germany from 1977 until the mid-1990s.[16]

Red Zora was a Marxist feminist offshoot of a group called the Revolutionary Cells. Red Zora launched dozens of firebomb attacks, mostly targeting unoccupied buildings they associated with imperialism, the criminalization of abortion, the exploitation of women workers, or the control or coercive commodification of women's bodies. In some of these attacks, the monkeywrenching logic of material sabotage recedes into the background in favour of a strictly symbolic or propagandistic approach. In other cases, the aim was explicitly to take buildings out of use, and at least in those cases of material destruction, Red Zora was clearly engaged in so-called citizen-saboteur militancy.

Red Zora's arson attacks were designed to avoid injuring people. This matters because, generally speaking, the danger with arson attacks is that they will unintentionally lead to bystander deaths or injuries. Respect for the value of common decency would rule out actions that could reasonably be expected to put blameless bystanders, such as families who live adjacent to targeted buildings, at grave risk of harm. Red Zora militants earnestly strove to keep bystanders safe:

> Because of the possibility of endangering life we are forced to be especially responsible.... It would be a paradox to struggle against a system for which life is only worthwhile as long as it is utilizable and at the same time to become as cynical and brutal as that system. There were many actions we rejected because we couldn't eliminate the danger to innocent people.[17]

This passage suggests – and I do not for a moment doubt – that they were very serious about accountability, in the sense of sensitivity to the democratic values of common decency and the common good, as part and parcel of the responsibilities of militants claiming democratic legitimacy for their actions.

It is worth noting how different this is from the kind of amoralism that openly scorns the standard of decency and respect for the safety of bystanders.[18] Although I insist on underlining the distance that separates Red Zora from such an approach, it is nevertheless a concern that the intention of a group of militants to refrain from endangering bystanders may not be enough. Ann Hansen, a prominent supporter of Red Zora whose own activism evidently sought to replicate some of its most striking features, recounts how an action that she helped organize went awry:

> By the fall of 1982, Direct Action decided to sabotage the [Toronto-area weapons manufacturing] Litton plant in an attempt to deter any further investment by the American mother plant and to cause significant financial damage to the plant itself. . . . Despite numerous precautions to avoid injuries . . . seven people were injured in the bombing.[19]

Among the injuries, mostly affecting security guards and factory workers, were broken bones, serious head injuries, and smoke inhalation. Fortunately, no one died, but one of the workers spent most of the next year in hospital.[20] Direct Action issued an apology and expressed various self-criticisms after the event.[21]

It seems inescapable that there is an element of unpredictability inherent in the use of explosives and fire, which makes it hard to rely on good intentions as a safeguard against unintended injuries. According to Direct Action, the Litton bomb "exploded twelve minutes too early."[22] When some members of the Weather Underground Organization tried to build a bomb inside a Greenwich Village home in 1970, they blew themselves up in what came to be known as the Townhouse Explosion.[23] Also in 1970, an anti-imperialist group exploded a bomb in a military research building at the University of Wisconsin at 3:40 a.m., only to learn later that a mathematics graduate student, unexpectedly present at that hour, died in the explosion.[24] By contrast, Red Zora injured no one. Is this because of their more careful planning and superior technical expertise for the safe use of tactical firebombing and explosive devices? Maybe. But the accountability principle would ask of militants at least the same level of technical expertise and caution in saboteur activities that one demands from businesses that use fire and explosives. It's not clear how often a semiclandestine radical-activist group can successfully approximate that standard, given the difficult conditions under which activists live and work.

Overall, I think that the main implication in the context of the accountability principle is to encourage citizen-saboteurs to steer clear of such volatile methods as firebombing and explosives, except under the most urgent circumstances, and when their confidence in the material (not just symbolic) efficacy of the tactic is very high. A tactic that might put bystanders in grave danger should almost never be undertaken anywhere near homes or workplaces. The likelihood of fire spreading to occupied buildings nearby seems too great a risk to take, especially if one endorses Red Zora's insistence that actions be rejected whenever danger to innocent people couldn't be eliminated. Sound militancy will thus show a systematic preference for forms of sabotage that minimize these risks.

Even so, it is not the fire or the property damage that should be of concern, but the failure to show due regard for the standards of common decency that were so well articulated by Red Zora.

Other Targets of Sabotage: Machinery and Roads

Sabotage-oriented antilogging organizers have not relied primarily on tree-spiking. A key tactic used against the logging industry has been the tactical damaging of construction machinery and roads, in the context of broader efforts to block logging projects. The same methods have been used, perhaps more extensively still, by saboteurs resisting urban-sprawl construction sites.[25]

Earth First!, the Earth Liberation Front, and the Animal Liberation

Front, among others, have used these methods against logging companies, animal research firms, oil and gas corporations, biotechnology companies, and others regarded as appropriate movement targets. These are a few examples:

- "A German group calling itself The Moles took up a railway line and dug tunnels under a road in an attempt to stop a nuclear convoy from travelling by either rail or road. The tunnels under the road were designed to allow normal vehicles to cross over the tunnels without any problem, but would collapse if they were driven over by a hundred ton nuclear convoy vehicle."[26]
- "Anonymous eco-activists used a loader to rip up 115 meters of railway track used by Weyerhaeuser mill in Grand Prairie, Alberta. They also crashed the loader into an electricity pole taking out the main power line."[27]
- "Activists in Spain cut the cables on machinery used to construct the controversial Itoiz dam, thereby delaying the project by a full 12 months."[28]
- According to a Mexican Earth Liberation Front communiqué issued on December 30, 2008, "an urban construction machine was sabotaged with most of the cables cut, leaving it unusable and blocking the street until they moved it by other means."[29]

Although all of these actions involve the destructive style of militancy, which provokes hostile condemnations from big business and harsh repression from the police, from a moral or a democratic-theoretical point of view, there is no reason to recoil from such measures. In effect, this type of sabotage, which simply disables machinery and equipment, normally poses no danger to anyone. What it does is cost people, or corporations, money. But that is exactly what strikes, consumer boycotts, and even negative publicity campaigns do. They cost targeted firms money. So the cynical attempt by law enforcement agencies and prosecutors to brand saboteurs of this type as "ecoterrorists" is both baseless and dangerous.[30]

Sabotage of this kind, which harms no one in a physical way, but simply imposes monetary burdens on corporations that may well be profiting from environmental injustice and ecological irresponsibility, could play the same kind of role that other forms of cost-raising protest play, namely, to offset the power asymmetries that make it hard for communities to push back against incursions by big corporations backed by big governments.

Is Democracy the Right Standard?

In the context of this book, the key question is whether the tactics of sabotage groups satisfy the criteria laid out in the democratic standard. It is worth noting, however, that practitioners of ecological sabotage would, for the most part, reject those criteria. The reason is that the democratic standard is, as they would put it, "humanist," or "anthropocentric." Many radical environmentalists, and almost all participants in groups like Earth First! and the Earth Liberation Front, consider themselves to be "biocentric" or "ecocentric" in their ethical perspectives. That is to say, they do not privilege the concerns or interests of human beings over the independent (noninstrumental) value and importance of animals and ecosystems.

Along with many other democratic theorists, including John Dryzek, Robin Eckersley, and Michael Saward, I believe that, in the long run, a deliberative-democratic theory of voice, like the one that underlies the democratic standard, could be developed in a form that would incorporate the most compelling insights of ecocentric moral thinking.[31] In this spirit, political philosophers Andrew Dobson and Kristian Skagen Ekeli have each argued that the disregard of both nonhuman animals and future generations of people in contemporary liberal-capitalist political and economic institutions can be addressed by broadening our notion of stakeholder voice to empower proxies for both animals and future generations (of humans and nonhumans).[32] Other democratic theorists, notably Dryzek, have argued that it is possible to think of ecosystems as communicating, for example, signalling distress in response to human activities that harm living systems. A genuinely deliberative-democratic polity, in that case, should be attentive and responsive to those signals, and take seriously the point of view that they make manifest.[33] From this point of view, arguably, militancy on behalf of other species and future generations could be described as a language of the unheard.[34]

Under the democratic standard, it is crucial that publics develop a way to understand the notion of common decency and the common good. I would argue that this is an open-ended notion, the content of which cannot be fully settled independently of and prior to public deliberation, but has to be settled in and through such deliberation. Thus, although the democratic standard is not ecocentric, it is arguably not anthropocentric either, in that it does not preclude understandings of common decency and the common good that are expansive enough to include other species and (more obviously) future generations. In essence, democratic publics have to take up the question of whose dignity and whose welfare matters, how much regard is due regard for the bearers of such dignity and/or welfare, and what institutional measures can be taken to ensure that democratic discussion is sufficiently inclusive to address all relevant points of view. The democratic standard's demand is that militants act only in ways that are defensible as duly sensitive to the democratic values of common decency and the common good. How other species, future generations, and ecosytems figure in these judgments is an open question.

Respect for Persons, Not for Property

Reflecting on the cases considered here, a pattern appears. Where saboteurs position themselves as above considerations of decency, that is, when they see no need to confine their conduct to actions that they could justify to others as consistent with common decency and the common good, then they go astray, endangering bystanders and weakening their claim to democratic legitimacy and civic virtue.

But when critics of these militants attack them for damaging property, they also miss the point. Damaging property – at least replaceable property, and especially corporate property – usually only costs others money. (For the most part, it costs insurance companies money, to be precise.) If that is the injurious part of the action, then it is neither more nor less injurious than costing people or businesses similar amounts of money by means of boycotts, picket lines, or other kinds of disruption. Instead, in reflecting upon the soundness of proposals to destroy property to advance the cause of justice, the important point is the moral importance of treating people decently. Property itself, in the types of case that are most relevant to the ethics of militant protest, is important only in the way that money is important. It is possible to harm people or institutions by costing them money. But it is not its own special kind of harm: it is the familiar practice of imposing costs on an adversary, to deincentivize intransigence and unresponsiveness. Often, it is admirable.

In short, it is to persons that we owe respect, not to their property. Where we cannot damage or destroy their property except by treating them indecently, our respect for the persons extends to their property. But if property damage does nothing worse than cost a corporation money, it is disingenuous to claim that such damage transgresses against the moral rights of any person.

Finally, let me underline that, if this insistence on the standard of common decency leads me to cast doubt on some tactical choices of some saboteurs, it is still more clear from this same standard that one should reject the state's campaign of persecution against justice-seeking civic organizations, under the flimsy pretext that their rigorously non-lethal tactics constitute ecoterrorism.[35] This "green scare," or demonization of ecologically motivated community organizations, has without doubt caused more harm than any of the groups or individuals persecuted in the course of it. For this reason, all environmentalists, civil libertarians, and defenders of democracy are duty-bound to close ranks in support of those victimized by the fake panic about threats posed by dissenters and protesters.

Sound militancy is an important civic virtue, and as such it requires communities to sustain and support the practice of cultivating, defending, and spreading that virtue. If the state, cynically doing the bidding of big business by trying to destroy the lives of people who stand up to corporations, is allowed to win in these battles, the ideal of public autonomy will be immeasurably weakened for a long time to come.

{ Seven }

The Black Bloc

In late June 2010, the G20 heads of government held a weekend summit in downtown Toronto, insulated from contact with protesters by levels of police repression that bordered on martial law. By the time the meetings had ended, more than 1,100 activists had been arrested in the largest wave of mass arrests in Canadian history. Most were released without ever having been charged; most of those who were charged were never convicted of anything. Many of the arrests were later judged by an independent police review to be "arbitrary and unlawful."[1] A few dozen activists were convicted of crimes, and some organizers were made to spend significant periods under house arrest or in prison. Most of these criminalized protesters were arrested on conspiracy charges prior to the main protest.[2] Arguably, most of the law-breaking that took place during the G20 summit consisted of crimes committed by police officers and other public officials, rather than by protesters.[3]

A series of quite dramatic, small-scale acts of property destruction were, however, undertaken by some attendees at the protest. Almost all of these acts were carried out by a loosely organized crowd of about 150 masked protesters dressed in black.[4] Together, they smashed the front windows of several banks, dozens of brand-name retail stores, and a large ground-floor window at Toronto's Police Headquarters, while also smashing up and torching a few police cars. Thousands of more or less stunned onlookers watched as the masked crowd wound its way through downtown Toronto, smashing window after window, oddly unchallenged by the thousands of riot police saturating the city centre. All in all, it made for quite a memorable spectacle. The next day, Toronto newspapers were filled with breathless commentary on the black-clad, masked protesters who had left such a shocking trail of property destruction in their wake. This was Toronto's first significant encounter with the notorious "black bloc" phenomenon.

What Is a Black Bloc?

In Part I, I held up the 1999 Seattle protest against the WTO as a turning point in the resurgence of militant protest in recent years. The Battle of Seattle was an exemplar of militancy as a civic virtue that promotes democratic inclusion and challenges intransigent elites and unresponsive systems of power. Although probably not the most important type and certainly not the most widespread, one of the most widely discussed types of militancy on display in Seattle was the appearance on the scene of a black bloc. The bloc was unfamiliar even to most of the seasoned activists at the Seattle protests, and it generated considerable debate. It also created many of the most memorable and sensational images that quickly captured public attention in the wake of the protests.

At times, journalistic commentators have mistaken the black bloc for some kind of anarchist organization, an interpretation so baseless that it can only be explained as a symptom of the indifference and scorn with which the bloc is viewed by such writers. More plausibly, some people who take an interest in it describe the black bloc as a tactic.[5] I, too, sometimes refer to it this way, but strictly speaking the black bloc is better thought of as a tactical formation.

When a black bloc is formed at a large-scale public demonstration, the question of what tactics the bloc will pursue remains to be answered. Will it focus on symbolic property destruction, such as window-breaking, as it did in Toronto in 2010?[6] Will it physically obstruct the police to deter arrests and repel police violence against protesters, as it did in Cairo in 2013?[7] Or will it attempt to breach police lines or fences established to limit the movements of protesters, as it did in Quebec City in

2001?[8] The fact that a bloc has been formed does not answer these questions.

In order to assess the role of black blocs as languages of the unheard, that is, as vehicles for fostering public autonomy and securing a voice for the silenced or ignored, it may matter crucially whether the bloc is going to attempt to repel police violence and mass arrests or, on the contrary, to evacuate the scene when police violence and arrests begin, melting away into the city. Blocs have adopted each of these responses at times. It is a disappointing feature of the way the bloc has been debated on the left that, again and again, people treat it as admissible to take a yes-or-no position on "the black bloc" as such, rather than first asking, A black bloc for what? The mistake of describing the bloc as a tactic, rather than as a formation for co-ordinated pursuit of a range of possible tactics, fuels the confusion and oversimplification that mars so many debates about this topic.

The black bloc formation typically entails the convergence of a number of protesters, usually ranging from a few dozen to a few hundred (on rare occasions in Europe, as many as a few thousand), dressed in black clothes, marching together as a more or less distinct group within a larger demonstration, covering their faces with masks or balaclavas. Often, participants carry sticks, rocks, or hammers. Once assembled, equipped, and marching in a tight group, bloc participants attempt to co-ordinate their actions in such a way as to maximize their capacity to engage in either effective street-fighting or attacks on symbolically significant corporate or government property (usually bank or retail store windows, but sometimes also police cars or police stations). One bloc participant has described it as "a temporary cohesive grouping with the immediate goal of creating a . . . street fighting force, which in practice would dissolve with the conclusion of the action at hand."[9] Among the activities that have been undertaken by black bloc formations within mass demonstrations are the breaking of store windows, attempts to breach police lines or tear down fences that limit the public's capacity to engage in protest activity, and the de-arresting of protesters who have been or are about to be taken into police custody.

The immediate aim of adopting the bloc formation is usually to make it possible to engage in such activities while ensuring anonymity to make arrests and criminal convictions more difficult. Some bloc participants attach significance to the mask as a symbol of solidarity.[10] But for most, the masks are mainly a practical convenience, to make repressive crackdowns more difficult. "Acting in a bloc is especially useful when some of the participants in the action expect they may break laws," according to one tactical manual. "When everyone in a group looks the same, it is difficult for the police or others to tell who did what."[11] In contrast to civil disobedience of the type promoted by Gandhi and King, bloc protesters do not normally favour allowing the police to arrest activists without obstruction or interference, so measures to evade arrest are deemed sensible and prudent.

The anonymity of black bloc protesters makes it impossible to confirm or disconfirm perceptions, stereotypes, or boasts about the demographic makeup or ideological affinities of bloc participants, but many people claim (rightly or wrongly) that bloc participants in North America are disproportionately young, disproportionately white, and disproportionately anarchist.[12] Whatever the veracity of these claims, I believe that no one would deny that there has been a close connection between anarchist conceptions of effective resistance and the use of black blocs, especially at major summit protests such as the ones in Toronto in 2010 or Seattle in 1999. Nevertheless, it is well-known that Maoists, autonomist Marxists, and other political currents also sometimes participate in black blocs, although in some cases these nonanarchists may refrain from donning black clothes or wearing masks. Variants of the bloc tactic include a socialist red bloc, an LGBTQ pink bloc, and a padded bloc of the kind once favoured by the Tute Bianche (White Overalls) in Italy, but I will confine my attention here to the schwarze Block in Germany and the black bloc in North America.

Before exploring the politics and the ethics of black bloc tactics, and assessing the soundness of black bloc protest according to the democratic standard, I should say a little to put the black bloc into historical context.

History of the Black Bloc

To many North American activists, the bloc has seemed like an innovation (for better or for worse) in protest tactics originating only in the late 1990s. And there is a grain of truth in this, at least in the sense that the full package of black bloc elements underwent a certain codification and standardization around fifteen years ago, when it first became popular within the protest culture of the United States and Canada. Since that time, the bloc has taken a specific, routinized form: the all-black clothes, the faces covered by bandanas or balaclavas, the functioning as a small, relatively disciplined formation, usually within a larger mass demonstration, and the close association of the tactic with anarchist views about the state. However, close observers agree that this standardized black bloc, which took its final shape in North America, was a conscious adaptation of a style of protest that had been pursued throughout the 1980s and 90s in Europe, especially in Germany. The German schwarze Block was invented by a militant strand of the West German far left that emerged at the end of the 1970s. Known as the Autonomists (*Autonomen*), they have been thought to resemble some strands of North American anarchism, but originally had some affinity with the Italian Autonomist Marxism of the 1970s.[13]

The first "official" black bloc in Germany was organized for a May Day march in Frankfurt, in 1980,[14] although even this was an attempt to reproduce a tactic that had been used by the German Autonomists against the police the previous year during a successful attempt to prevent neo-Nazis from holding a march.[15] Because the tactic was seen to have been effective, and because police violence against peaceful protesters in West Germany at the time cried out for a forceful response, the new approach was quickly embraced by a section of the radical left, which began to promote the tactic and the "black bloc" name in radical publications as early as 1981. Politically, many German radicals saw the bloc innovation as a suitable correction to the passivity and incapacity to grapple with police repression that then plagued the Gandhi-influenced mainstream antiwar movement.[16]

The very real differences between the typical German bloc in the

1980s and the typical North American black bloc of recent years are worth noting, to the extent that the aesthetic dimension of the bloc has been foregrounded by those who regard the bloc as primarily expressive or theatrical. The German variant of the bloc tactic, at least in the 1980s, had a more irregular appearance: not only black clothes, for instance, and as many motorcycle and construction helmets as masks and balaclavas (a feature that led the West German state to disallow anyone other than police officers from wearing helmets at demonstrations). The early German blocs seem to have been more pragmatic than expressive, so that the aesthetic aspect – or what one bloc advocate calls "the mystique of the Black Bloc" as "a powerful propaganda image"[17] – played a less important role. Nevertheless, there is no mistaking the continuities. The core elements were all there: the mostly dark clothing, the covered faces to ensure anonymity, the sticks, rocks, and clubs, the functioning as a physically tight and disciplined formation, usually (but not always) marching within a larger group, and the tendency to engage in street-fighting against the police (or neo-Nazis) and window-breaking directed against corporate or government targets.

It took more than a decade for the importation of the bloc tactic into North America to unfold. In January 1991, a now-defunct anarchist federation, Love and Rage, called for what they explicitly called a "black bloc" contingent to participate in a mass demonstration in Washington, DC, against the Persian Gulf War.[18] During the march, the black bloc contingent broke off temporarily from the main march to smash windows at the headquarters of the World Bank and the US Treasury building, hoping to draw attention to the link between global capitalism and US war policy. They then rejoined the main march and apparently avoided any arrests.[19] The perception of success encouraged imitation, especially in the antifascist movement, which was all the more receptive because it was the section of the activist left in North America with the closest ties to grassroots protest culture in Continental Europe.

But it was in Seattle that the bloc tactic burst into the consciousness of radical activists in Canada and the United States. The bloc in Seattle consisted of only about 250 people among tens of thousands of protesters in Seattle that weekend.[20] Yet the visual images it produced took on an importance far greater than one might have expected. Two types of images were especially important: first, mainstream news media highlighted several images of bloc participants smashing windows of stores and banks; and second, activists themselves took note of scenes in which bloc members were confronted by a few other protesters who tried physically to prevent them from breaking windows. The controversy generated by these images greatly magnified the bloc's impact on the Seattle events and their aftermath.

It is fair to say that the black bloc has become one of the most controversial protest tactics among activists in Canada and the United States. It is also fair to say that it has had a polarizing effect. Some activists embrace it as a useful form of militancy; others reject it on moral grounds because it violates their conception of nonviolence. Still others reject it on largely strategic grounds, as a tactic that weakens the capacity of movements to broaden their base of participation because it creates entry barriers for nonradicals within the wider working class.

Criticisms of Black Blocs

By and large, critics of black blocs make one or more of three criticisms. First, there is the most popular complaint, that blocs are violent rather than nonviolent. Second, there is the complaint that they are self-indulgent rather than solidaristic. And finally, there is the complaint that black blocs are self-defeating rather than strategically effective. Although each of these objections has a different emphasis, ultimately they all point toward the same basic worry: that the black bloc persistently fails to live up to the democratic standard's opportunity principle, notably its emphasis on creating new opportunties to resolve important grievances.

The violence complaint is given an eloquent articulation by San Francisco–based writer Rebecca Solnit, in her article "Throwing Out the Master's Tools, and Building a Better House." According to Solnit, many of the tactics typical of the bloc are violent, and violence tends to undermine what is most subversive and transformative about the movements into which bloc protest intrudes. “The state would like us to be violent,” she says. “Violence as cooptation tries to make us more like them, and if we're like them they win twice – once because being unlike them is our goal and again because then we're then easier to imprison, brutalize, marginalize, etc.” But her objection is not rooted in a strict pacifist rejection of all political violence. She concedes that political violence is sometimes legitimate: “I'm more than fine with the ways the Zapatista rebels in southern Mexico have defended themselves and notice how sadly necessary it sometimes is, and I sure wouldn't dictate what Syrians or Tibetans may or may not do.” Instead, she objects to bloc violence largely because she believes it works against the aims that bloc participants are attempting to advance. In particular, because the bloc's violence is coercive and violates the bodily integrity of its targets, it is authoritarian and encourages elitist behaviours. And because it is both dangerous and unpopular, it narrows the base of participation in movements, which isolates radicals from the wider population and thereby insulates elites from the threat posed by broad-based movements with transformative aspirations. “So when episodes of violence break out as part of our side in a demonstration, an uprising, a movement, I think of it as a sabotage, a corruption, a coercion, a misunderstanding, or a mistake, whether it's a paid infiltrator or a clueless dude.”[21]

The complaint that the bloc is self-indulgent is one of the objections offered by left-wing journalist and author Chris Hedges in his notorious rant against the bloc's role in the Occupy movement, in which he described the bloc, rather provocatively, as “the cancer in Occupy.” According to Hedges's interpretation, the black bloc is a type of acting out that is both tactically pointless (or worse) and psychologically immature.

> The Black Bloc movement is infected with a deeply disturbing hypermasculinity.... Marching as a uniformed mass, all dressed in black to become part of an anonymous bloc, faces covered, temporarily overcomes alienation, feelings of inadequacy, powerlessness and loneliness. It imparts to those in the mob a sense of comradeship. It permits an inchoate rage to be unleashed on any target. Pity, compassion and

> tenderness are banished for the intoxication of power. It is the same sickness that fuels the swarms of police who pepper-spray and beat peaceful demonstrators. It is the sickness of soldiers in war. It turns human beings into beasts.[22]

This outburst from Hedges and the larger rant from which it is drawn are so overstated as to be unconvincing even to fierce critics of the bloc. This is especially true of his taunting reference to cancers to be removed and his identification of bloc activists as both criminals and *agents provocateurs* working for the police. Nevertheless, underlying the rhetoric is an objection that seems worth airing, if only because it articulates a widely shared opinion. At the heart of Hedges's complaint is the claim that black blocs tend to be self-indulgent. Specifically, they address the psychological need for self-expression or acting out on the part of bloc participants, rather than the political-strategic needs of the movements into which they insert themselves. For instance, even bloc advocates have been known to insist that blocs serve to vent feelings of rage, to convey sentiments of revulsion against capitalism or consumerism, or to imbue frustrated young radicals with a subjective sense of efficacy and momentary triumph.[23] To the extent that these experiences of potency and possibility work to dissolve widespread feelings of alienation and marginalization among young radicals, these might be laudable effects. But what if, as Hedges thinks, bloc activists seek out these psychological satisfactions by participating in protests in a manner that undermines the intended effect of the larger action? That would presumably be a sort of personal failing: a self-indulgent elevation of one's own psychological needs above the needs of the movement one purports to be aiding. It would be unsound militancy.

To the objections of Solnit and Hedges, we may add the third complaint, that black blocs are self-defeating. This is the accusation of influential radical environmentalist Derrick Jensen, who is quoted at substantial length in Hedges's article. According to Jensen, the problem with bloc activists is that they are wilfully unresponsive or indifferent to strategic considerations, and for this reason they persistently act in ways that set the movement back rather than moving it forward. He sees bloc activism as a type of transgressive performance, which attempts to create an exhilarating and defiant spectacle. What it does not do, he suggests, is choose tactics based on sound and careful judgment about what combination of actions would best advance the movement in the present context.

> Their thinking is not only nonstrategic, but actively opposed to strategy. They are unwilling to think critically about whether one is acting appropriately in the movement. I have no problem with someone violating boundaries [when] that violation is the smart, appropriate thing to do. I have a huge problem with people violating boundaries for the sake of violating boundaries. It is a lot easier to pick up a rock and throw it through the nearest window than it is to organize, or at least figure out which window you should throw a rock through if you are going to throw a rock. A lot of it is laziness.[24]

In Jensen's judgment, bloc participants are unwilling to do the difficult work of analyzing the complex dynamics of the movement in the present conjuncture. Sound militancy, according to Jensen, looks for strategic openings to move the struggle forward; it strengthens the resistance and undermines the movement's adversaries by effectively deploying well-chosen and timely tactics. But bloc activists neglect this work to the point of irresponsibility. According to Jensen's interpretation, this neglect flows from the assumption that spectacular upheavals, like clashes with the police or the shattering of retail storefronts, are self-justifying, regardless of the strategic implications in particular contexts.

What unites the complaints from Solnit, Hedges, and Jensen is a shared concern that the black bloc tactic simply does not work. In the language of the democratic standard, the concern is that blocs do nothing to create opportunities for the resolution of important grievances.

Three Faces of the Black Bloc

Defenders of the bloc do have responses to offer to these objections about its alleged strategic ineffectiveness. Occasionally, these responses can seem laughable or embarrassing. One winces to read, in CrimethInc.'s *Recipes for Disaster*, that "a bloc might attempt to set off full-scale rioting, in hope of precipitating an insurrection."[25] But often the defences conveyed are more serious, and attempt to offer plausible strategic rationales for the practice. Three of the most important ascribed contributions are the performative, the pedagogical, and the protective functions of black blocs.

Performative Blocs

One of the most intriguing suggestions offered in defence of black blocs is that they have an important performance value. According to this view, blocs are justified on what one might call dramaturgical grounds, as a kind of staging or expressive display. Anarchist Chuck Munson has described the bloc as "the anarchist equivalent of a gay pride march."[26] In this version of what the bloc contributes, it is seen as a kind of quasi-theatrical communication, useful to social movements because it helps to project important images. Its "aim is primarily symbolic and concerned with political communication," and it "lets a political actor signify here and now her or his critique of an immoral system."[27]

The bloc action in Toronto in 2010, for example, appeared mainly to be performative in character. Often, window-breaking is the tell-tale indicator that a bloc's tactical orientation is dramaturgical, that is, that its primary activity is to stage a public spectacle or performance. Black blocs do not generally loot. Certainly, there was very little looting (and probably none by bloc participants) in the Toronto G20 events. And most activists are too sophisticated to think that petty window-breaking by black blocs will somehow cripple the insurance industry, with its $3.2 trillion in annual revenues.[28] So the bloc's window-breaking in Toronto appears to have been mainly an activity of orchestrated image-making, prepared for public viewing.

Pedagogical Blocs

A somewhat different function is served by what I call a pedagogical black bloc. Whereas the performative bloc is mainly oriented toward the public expression of feelings, opinions, or allegiances deemed by protesters to be worthy of public display, the pedagogical bloc is more other-regarding. Its aim is popular education. The contrast is akin to that between hoisting a flag in a public square versus offering to explain its significance to onlookers.

The pedagogical theme is developed in some detail by Jeff Shantz in his 2011 book, *Active Anarchy*, although at times he blurs the line between the performative and the pedagogical.[29] Shantz argues that the bloc, as a form of critical popular education, pursues the classical anarchist strategy of "propaganda of the deed." Pedagogical blocs, he says, can have the effect of weakening the grip of ruling-class ideologies. The idea is "that exemplary acts against representatives of the state and capital might serve as pedagogical tools in the processes of de-legitimizing bourgeois morality and encouraging the oppressed to shed such ingrained values as respect for property and the law." Witnessing a small but determined group defying and confronting the property of the rich and the laws and brutality of the state, and getting away with it, emboldens observers to throw off their usual habits of deference to power. The effect on some, Shantz suggests, is a "shattering of hegemonic corporate claims on ownership and property rights which are deeply ingrained but . . . illegitimate."[30] Essentially, a bloc serves this pedagogical function if it serves to unmask the system as, on the one hand, coercive and undemocratic, and on the other hand, vulnerable to defiance and contestation.

An example of a pedagogical bloc would be the black bloc in Pittsburgh at the 2009 G20 heads of government summit. The bloc actions there were relatively uneventful, with some of the usual clashes with police and some property damage. But the sense of purpose that animitated that bloc was pedagogical in a specific way. It was, in the words of one bloc participant in Pittsburgh, an assertion of "the survival of militant street resistance in the Obama era."[31] In other words, it was an attempt by some radicals to reassert the importance of a confrontational stance toward the state, in a time when sections of the activist world in the US were moving toward the Democratic Party and a (short-lived, as it turned out) revival of optimism about the official political process. By drawing out the state into a confrontation, and defying police orders to disperse, the bloc attempted to remove a public relations mask from the state, and to reveal its coercive and undemocratic nature. The gulf separating the state from the people became impossible to overlook. In this way, the bloc went beyond dramaturgy and tried to intervene in the left activist scene with an educative contribution.

Protective Blocs

The third function is that of the protective bloc, which plays either of two related roles: deterring or repelling police brutality and repression, or defending the right or capacity to protest in public. This is perhaps the least sensational function for a bloc, but it is also the oldest, since the early European blocs were overwhelmingly focused on providing protective functions. They fought off police attacks to defend squatters from eviction, they deterred or repelled police attempts to arrest or disperse marchers, and they tried to break through police lines to reclaim public space from police control.[32]

It is not a relic of a bygone era, however. Two post-Seattle examples come to mind: the black bloc in Quebec City, at the Summit of the Americas in 2001, and the black blocs in Cairo, Egypt, in and around Tahrir Square in 2013. In Quebec City, the bloc was protective in both senses. There were numerous attempts by the bloc to de-arrest people or prevent arrests in advance, as well as more generally to insulate marchers from the full effect of police brutality by confronting the police tactically. The Quebec City bloc also tried to defend the right or capacity to mount public resistance. Most notably, they did this by successfully tearing down metal fences erected by police to deny or limit the right to protest in certain public spaces. Many of the other protesters and city residents reportedly appreciated the bloc's protective functions.[33]

In Cairo, the blocs that emerged intermittently in 2013 reportedly played what one could perhaps call a security role, keeping police away from protests and intervening to prevent violence against women protesters.[34]

Do Black Blocs Make a Strategic Contribution?

One limitation of most debates about the bloc is that all sides seem to assume that one should either be for or against something called "the black bloc." But there is no reason to think that the strategic efficacy of black blocs should be the same for blocs of all three varieties. It may very well be that some types of bloc are more vulnerable to criticism than others. Let's consider them one by one.

To the extent that we can isolate in practical contexts the performative function from the pedagogical and the protective (which, I concede, is easier said than done), the blocs pursuing the performative function are the most vulnerable to the critics' objections. After all, their aim is not so much to offer potency or efficacy to social movements, but instead to offer visibility and self-expression to the activists whose performances comprise the staged spectacle. Hedges's charge of self-indulgence seems particularly telling against the performative approach. To be sure, performative blocs play a role or function. They are not mindless or random outbursts. But their function is fundamentally self-regarding, a contribution that the bloc makes to its own participants. It benefits them, by serving as a vehicle for their public self-expression, but not necessarily their supposed movement allies.

Critics' concerns over the performative aspects of the black bloc seem well-founded. Performative blocs really do neglect the importance of creating opportunities to resolve important grievances for larger movements. If they were conducted separately, away from other protesters' demonstrations, the objection would be less compelling, as I argue below. But Solnit, Hedges, and Jensen assume a model of the bloc as a type of tactical intervention within wider movements and larger demonstrations. When blocs intervene in broader struggles, they thereby acquire a responsibility to offer something, or at least to refrain from interfering with or scuttling the plans of others. If a bloc is likely to affect other protesters, either by inviting physical confrontations with the police or by upstaging the intended messages and effects that nonbloc organizers aim to produce, the question of how the bloc affects fellow protesters would be paramount. But the performative approach to blocs seems to treat these side effects as a matter of little or no importance, because they do not figure in the dramaturgy of the main spectacle.

The opportunity principle insists that militancy should create opportunties to overcome elite intransigence or unresponsive systems of power, in order to advance the resolution of important grievances. That principle would steer activists away from performative blocs, at least when they seem likely to interfere with the aims of nonbloc protesters by distracting from messages or encouraging police confrontations. The other two types of bloc are less obviously vulnerable to this line of attack.

A pedagogical bloc attempts to offer something to movements which everyone agrees they need, and that is popular education. Anyone can understand why activist critical pedagogy or radical education can make a strategic contribution to social-change movements. However, the propaganda-of-the-deed analysis of how blocs can play an educational role has a major defect. In order for the propaganda of the deed to be effective, bold acts of small-group defiance would have to actually convey to onlookers either that the state or the capitalist order is weaker than it looks, or that acts of defiance can produce unexpectedly favourable results. If either point were the likely conclusion drawn by onlookers to bloc actions, then the black bloc tactical formation could plausibly be said to have a useful pedagogical role in dissolving the habits of deference or compliance that discourage broad-based anticapitalist resistance.

This, I believe, is how adovocates of the pedagogical bloc see things. One bloc advocate depicted the Toronto G20 bloc as having just such effects.[35] The police, he claimed, were exposed as incompetent and cowardly. The several thousand riot police stationed only blocks away proved no match for the "150 strong" black bloc. The police made no attempt to arrest bloc members because they were paralyzed by indecision and fear, and could not handle the tactical cleverness of the bloc, associated by the author with the tactical wisdom of Sun Tzu's *Art of War.*

The problem with this picture is that so few people find it credible. I do not doubt that bloc participants feel that they won the day in Toronto at the G20, because the police, for whatever reason, did not intervene against them. But this leaves out the most glaring aspect of what happened. After the small black bloc of about 150 participants had smashed several dozen windows, over a period of about forty-five minutes, the bloc disbanded and melted away into the city. With the bloc long gone, the police saw the opportunity to proceed with a wave of mass arrests. They met virtually no resistance. Observers cannot fail to have noted that the bloc did nothing to stop the 1,100 arrests, nor to stop the rampage of police brutality against protesters. Far from appearing weak and ineffectual, the state was given a free hand to stage a performance of its own, displaying its capacity to crack down on dissent unchecked by any apparent legal limits. The incapacity of the bloc or the rest of the activist community to deter or limit the state's crackdown was all too visible. It is hard to imagine that a significant number of people looked at this exchange and drew the conclusion that the state was weaker than the bloc, or that the state was vulnerable to bold confrontational action. On the contrary, an obvious conclusion was that the activist left, including the bloc, was vastly outmatched in strength and power by the totalitarian reach of the security state and the brutality of its riot police when the powers that be chose to unleash these weapons.

The problem, more generally, with the propaganda-of-the-deed analysis is that it both reflects and encourages an underestimation of the material roots of capitalist power. The systems of power and elite governance that block the path to justice and public autonomy are not invulnerable to challenge from below. But neither are they paper tigers, ready to be exposed by the bold actions of a small group as fragile and easily defeated, so that we can expect bloc actions to inspire others to join the fight until resistance begins to spread like a prairie fire. The naïveté of such hopes is all too evident. If the prairie fire scenario were plausible, the pedagocial interpretation of the bloc project would make an important strategic contribution. Unfortunately, it is not.

On the contrary, the core issue with which militant resistance must grapple is that the protracted intransigence of elites and the relentless unresponsiveness of systems of power show no sign of being easily overturned. The adversaries that activists confront are, if anything, more resilient and more ruthless and brutal when their power is endangered than most people understand. Time and again, leftists have underestimated the staying power and the tenacity of systems of domination and exploitation. A strategic orientation that aims at initiating far-reaching and fundamental social transformation must grapple with this problem, and that means that it must identify a plausible source of social power that can serve to counteract the formidable combination of economic and political power of big business and the state. To the extent that the pedagogical bloc relies on a propaganda-of-the-deed rationale, it is bound to be unconvincing, and the effect will be to reinforce objections rooted in the considerations that the opportunity principle underlines, namely the need to create and to seize opportunities for movement successes.

I do not discount the possibility that other interpretations of how blocs can play an important popular education role may be available.[36] But the more realistic these interpretations are, the more modest will be the claimed impacts. And as the list of benefits becomes both more realistic and shorter, the pedagogical bloc will tend to look less and less useful, when weighed against some of the costs of bloc confrontations, including divisive movement debates and sometimes adverse legal consequences for individual activists.

The third face of the black bloc, the protective bloc, is the easiest to defend in terms of autonomous democracy. Protective blocs straightforwardly serve the militant's vocation. By weakening the state's capacity to silence resisters, protective blocs amplify the voice of the voiceless. The protective bloc presents a more appealing and broadly acceptable interpretation of the role of bloc formations as offering a kind of public service: materially defending the capacity to protest and fending off the repression of the police. From the point of view of the democratic standard, the protective interpretation of the black bloc makes all the difference. Actions like window-breaking and other nonstrategic forms of symbolic property destruction offer very little, beyond a propaganda message, to the wider movement. In the protective interpretation of the bloc, such activities would be seen as unhelpful to the bloc's main function, because they divert the bloc from its primary role of defending the practical capacity to resist in the face of a hostile and aggressive state. Protective, public-service black blocs have good reason to focus their efforts on the hard but important work of repelling police violence, deterring mass arrests, and overcoming police barriers and blockades. Clearly, these behaviours are indicators of civic virtue, and the critiques of Solnit, Hedges, and Jensen miss the mark as applied to protective blocs.

These reflections point to the conclusion that it is not plausible to join either the bloc rejectionists (like Solnit, Hedges, and Jensen), nor the bloc proponents (like Graeber, Shantz, and Gelderloos), in adopting an across-the-board verdict. Rather, the democratic standard insists that one embrace the bloc when it serves a democratic role, as a language of the unheard that gives voice to the voiceless, but steer clear of it when it indulges in fruitless performance, offering nothing that would facilitate or hasten much-needed social transformations.

In practical terms, it makes good sense, from a moral and a strategic point of view, to encourage black blocs to adopt a protective interpretation of their role on the left and, accordingly, to encourage an emphasis on defending access to the right to protest and repelling police attacks and arrests, rather than an emphasis on symbolic property destruction. In this form, black blocs can play an important democratic role. While Solnit, Hedges, and Jensen are right about the criterion for judging black blocs – whether or not they help movements win – they go too far when they suggest that the black bloc always has to indulge in high-cost, low-benefit tactics. Sometimes blocs act in ways that minimize the costs (acrimony and repression) while maximizing the benefits (thwarting repression and defending the right to resist). These considerations should encourage a political rapprochement or mutual adjustment, wherein the bloc is accepted as having a legitimate and important role to play within social movements, and bloc participants themselves accept that they have to be accountable to the wider left for how their actions affect other protesters.

Unembedded Blocs

Most of the discussion in this chapter has assumed that black blocs operate as distinct contingents embedded within larger protest events. For instance, the black bloc in the Battle of Seattle consisted of a relatively small group of a few hundred people, within a much larger protest that drew in many thousands of demonstrators. Blocs that are embedded in this way are particularly controversial, because the actions of bloc participants can affect the capacity of other protesters to convey messages that they deem important, and can sometimes expose nonbloc protesters to a heightened risk of police violence or arbitrary arrest. This was the type of bloc that Solnit, Hedges, and Jensen were complaining about.

But not all black blocs are embedded in this way. Unembedded blocs, which function as separate demonstrations rather than as contingents within larger protests, are not altogether uncommon. They are particularly widespread in Europe, but they also occur in North America occasionally. For example, the largely pedagogical black bloc at the Pittsburgh G20, mentioned above, carried out an independent march consisting entirely of the bloc and its supporters. At the Toronto G20 protest, the bloc began as a contingent within a large demonstration with thousands of protesters organized by the Canadian Labour Congress, but near the end of that action separated itself from the main protest to lead a preannounced breakaway march (within which the bloc constituted the largest identifiable grouping), thereby partially de-embedding what began as a fully embedded bloc. Were all black blocs unembedded, the tactic would probably be far less controversial, because it would affect other protesters to a much more limited extent.

Do the objections raised by Solnit, Hedges, and Jensen still apply to unembedded black blocs? I think the answer is, for the most part, that they do not. At the very least, they apply with far less force. In particular, a performative bloc, which engages in dramaturgically motivated property destruction, can still be faulted for being ineffective as a movement-building tactic. But as long as it does nothing to interfere with the protest actions of others, and does not burden nonbloc protesters with a heightened and unwelcome risk of arrest or other forms of police repression, an unembedded performative bloc seems unlikely to impose significant costs on any protesters other than bloc members themselves. The main reason given above for encouraging black bloc participants to emphasize the protective function of blocs is that, in this way, the bloc could offer something helpful to other protesters, while minimizing the burdens it imposes on them. But since an unembedded bloc imposes far fewer burdens, it has less need to worry about offering benefits or providing services to the movements with which it engages.

However, there is a reason that the majority of black blocs in North America are embedded, rather than unembedded. It is that, unlike in Europe where a bloc can sometimes muster thousands of participants, North American blocs tend to number in the range of a hundred to five hundred and only very rarely exceed the thousand-participant mark. The smaller scale of blocs in the US and Canada make them much more vulnerable to police attacks and pre-emptive arrests than they would be in some European countries. By embedding a bloc within a larger protest event, the bloc formation gains additional room for manoeuvre, making it harder for the police to disperse or contain it at the beginning of a march. For this reason, there is a strong incentive for bloc activists in North America to continue their usual practice of opting to operate within large-scale mass protests, rather than as unembedded blocs. And this, in turn, underlines the importance of the judgment offered above: that black bloc activists should be encouraged to emphasize the protective function, rather than the performative and pedagogical functions, of the bloc formation.

{ Eight }

Rioting

ALTHOUGH MARTIN LUTHER KING's description of rioting as a language of the unheard serves as this book's guiding idea, King would no doubt reject my democratic standard. He uses the criterion of nonviolence to distinguish sound from unsound militancy. My standard, on the other hand, discourages forms of protest only if they show too little regard for the value of public autonomy.

In both views, of course, there is a normative contrast to be drawn. One cannot credibly claim that everything that goes on in the course of every act of confrontational protest is sound. Even amoralism (examined in chapter two) holds that resistance is not legitimate unless it ultimately serves moral ends; the militancy of neo-Nazis, for example, would be rejected as normatively unsound by amoralists of the left. The question is where, not whether, to draw the line. But the need to distinguish between sound and unsound forms of protest is especially acute in the matter of rioting, because during a riot, due to the recklessness or irresponsibility of some participants, real harms may wrongly be inflicted on some people for no good reason. In the most intense and confrontational riots, blameless bystanders can end up beaten, dispossessed, or even dead.

That a form of resistance might well lead blameless bystanders to be beaten or killed could stand as a good reason to disavow indulgence in it, especially when other options are available that might be both more effective and less dangerous to bystanders. And yet, holding fast to the importance of public autonomy, King's observation should discourage a too-hasty dismissal of rioting as always off limits. In some cases – and I would argue in many cases – rioting may serve as a vehicle for fostering social inclusion and civic equality. Rioting has a unique capacity to allow the voiceless to interrupt what King used to call "business as usual"[1] with a dramatic outbreak of autonomous refusal. Motivated by moral insight into the unfairness of their situation, and frustrated by intransigent elites and unresponsive institutions that ignore their grievances and thwart their aspirations, the unheard may sometimes find their voice in acts of collective defiance and confrontation. In this respect, rioting is not that different from other styles of militant resistance.

From Riots to Rioting

Rioting does sometimes entail harms to bystanders that are difficult or impossible to defend. Even more commonly, it involves acts of property damage that are, like sabotage or other forms of destruction, controversial. However, it would be a mistake to regard rioting mainly through the stereotyped lens of the most sensational rioting behaviours. Sometimes rioters do engage in burning cars and looting. Sometimes they assault individuals or damage property. Almost always, they clash with the police to one degree or another. But a one-sided fixation on these aspects of some riots makes it unnecessarily difficult to grasp the role that rioting can play in democratic politics, when it is done well.

Consider the case of the Stonewall Riot, in Greenwich Village, in June 1969. Today, with the benefit of hindsight, most people concede its democratic significance.[2] The rioting erupted in response to a police raid on a mafia-owned gay bar. The events and their impact are concisely summarized by radical journalist Andrew Kopkind:

> A bunch of drag queens and their friends pulled from the Stonewall bar in a police raid refused to go docilely into the paddy wagons and all hell broke loose along Christopher Street and in adjoining parks and alleys. Fighting between the queers and the cops resumed the next

> night, but that was the extent of the violence. And yet the Stonewall riot must count as a transformative moment of liberation, not only for homosexuals, who were the street fighters, but for the entire sexual culture, which broke out of confinement that night as surely as gay people emerged from the closet.[3]

In the Stonewall rioting, rocks were thrown at the police, windows were smashed, at least one car was overturned, and some garbage cans were set on fire.[4] But whatever reaction one has to these details, they should not be allowed to obscure the fact that Stonewall represented a powerful outbreak of public autonomy, signalling – as sound militancy so often does – that "here, the people rule."

Still, a normative conception of militancy like the democratic standard has to be brought to bear in order to separate the democratic from the undemocratic aspects of rioting. If controversial or questionable actions occur in riots, one should either defend them, when they are defensible, or condemn them, when they are not. But judging actions within a riot is not the same as judging a riot as a whole.

Often, one can judge a tactic or action holistically, because it is organized by a single group with an explicit plan, and it unfolds, if not entirely as planned, at least in a way that has been shaped by the choices and risks knowingly undertaken by the organizers. For instance, a planned and co-ordinated action, like the March on Washington in 1963[5] or even the Days of Rage in 1968,[6] can be meaningfully assessed as a unitary political event and judged to be admirable or not, depending on the circumstances and relevant features of the action. By contrast, most riots are not suitable for this kind of holistic assessment, because they are not actions carried out by a group, but events that unfold in an unplanned, unco-ordinated way, in which individuals may join or leave the riot freely, animated by their own personal aims and priorities. Indeed, it is typical at least of large-scale riots that they involve a range of actors with widely diverging motives and agendas. Some may join the riot with what they regard as a righteous motive, to challenge the legal order for its complicity with injustice. Others, however, may join opportunistically, sensing a rare chance to carry out revenge fantasies against an ethnic group they despise, in a context where consequences are likely to be minimal. It would be improper to offer a unitary assessment of these very different kinds of behaviour. On the contrary, one should not let admiration for the civic virtue of the first group excuse the racism and brutality of the second group. Conversely, one should not allow the rioting militants who challenge the authorities on behalf of substantive and pressing grievances to be stigmatized by a false association with the actions of people whose participation is steered by a completely different set of aims.

These considerations dictate that rioting as an activity, rather than riots as events, will be the focus of this chapter. Strictly speaking, it is not the Stonewall Riot that was admirable, but the actions of those who protested for justice during that riot. Perhaps every single rioter acted admirably. But if a few did not, and one or two shouted racist or anti-Semitic slurs or beat up a Muslim onlooker out of scorn for their religion, the appropriate response would be to condemn this wrongdoing without allowing it to discredit the conduct of the other rioters.

If the task is to apply the democratic standard to rioting behaviours, the first step must be to identify the nature of rioting. Only with a definition in hand can we take up the question of how it can be done well.

What Is Rioting?

In our use of this word, "rioting," we need to proceed with caution. As a legal concept, rioting originated within the realm of law enforcement; it has long been understood from the crime-control (or at least crowd-control) perspective of the police and the courts. In this usage, the word conjures up images of unruly mobs acting irrationally and threatening their neighbours, reflecting the term's roots in the concerns of the authorities, notably the worry that public order may be under threat.

This public order discourse on rioting has remained substantially unchanged for centuries. A 1683 British jurisprudential tract by Thomas Ellwood, entitled *A Discourse Concerning Riots*, offers a definition of rioting that is remarkably similar to contemporary legal definitions. A riot is underway, Ellwood tells us,

> when three persons, or more, are assembled together in arms, with a fore-intent and purpose to do such an unlawful act, as is both evil in itself, and hurtful to another, either in person, or estate; and do it in a forcible manner, to the apparent breach or disturbance of the peace, either by threatening words, show of armour, turbulent gesture, or open violence, and to the manifest terror of the people.[7]

Ellwood bases this definition on the common law standards of seventeenth-century Britain. The understanding of rioting in contemporary British law, and indeed in Canadian[8] and American[9] law as well, is essentially unchanged. For example, Britain's Public Order Act of 1986, section 1, states:

> Where 12 or more persons who are present together use or threaten unlawful violence for a common purpose and the conduct of them (taken together) is such as would cause a person of reasonable firmness present at the scene to fear for his personal safety, each of the persons using unlawful violence for the common purpose is guilty of riot.[10]

One feature shared by Ellwood's definition and those of contemporary legal systems is an emphasis on the possibility that rioting might harm or threaten either persons or property ("hurtful . . . in person, or estate"). The fixation on the idea of violence, including the motivated ambiguity of that word, which blurs the distinction between property damage and attacks on people, is typical of public order legal discourse. This discourse is frequently calculated to make the option of discretion or arbitrary criminalization available to the authorities. Also typical of the public order view of rioting is Ellwood's depiction of rioters as threatening or scary. In this usage, to be labelled a rioter is to be accused of some kind of wrongdoing or misconduct. Rioting is understood as a specifically sinister and disreputable form of civic engagement. The very use of the word implies the propriety of a police crackdown.

Because the public order discourse is so thoroughly informed by the concerns of crowd control and policing, I cannot here adopt this classical conception of the nature of rioting. On the contrary, the democratic standard highlights the possibility that rioting can sometimes serve as a vehicle for the excluded to push their grievances into a public sphere ordinarily closed to their contributions. For this reason, I seek a way of thinking and talking about rioting that is informed by a different set of concerns, namely, those of autonomous democracy and democratic politics.

Fortunately, another discourse about riots is available: a public autonomy discourse on the nature and merits of unruly crowds. Rioting is sometimes depicted, above all by historians, as an assertive but essentially admirable vehicle for the excluded and the ignored to insert their own priorities and demands into a public realm that would otherwise be dominated by unaccountable elites. Historians like George Rudé, E.J. Hobsbawm, and E.P. Thompson offer a view of rioters not as out-of-control mobs motivated by irrational rage, but as morally motivated defenders of community standards of common decency and the common good. According to this view, rioters defend democratic values against precisely the sort of intransigent elites and unresponsive systems of power (notably, state bureaucracies and capitalist markets) to which the public autonomy view of democracy attaches such importance.[11] The rioting crowd, as described by these historians, has the merit of replacing the cartoonish depiction of rioters as crazed mobs with a more nuanced depiction that acknowledges the crowd's capacity for angry confrontation, but also notes its capacity to be motivated by a sense of justice and to make discriminating judgments about whom or what to target. This picture of rioters is both more realistic and more helpful for elucidating a moral basis for sound rioting.

Of course, even a discriminating and rational rioter may also at times act in horrific and brutal (albeit still nonrandom) ways. Some rioters may go terribly astray, choosing the wrong targets and surrendering any claim to democratic legitimacy. To cite only one instance, some participants in a massive riot in Jakarta, Indonesia, in 1998 engaged in racist violence against Chinese people living in the city, including brutal sexual violence against Chinese women.[12] For this group of rioters (a small minority, it must be said, of the tens of thousands of participants), misogyny and ethnic bigotry informed their choice of targets and discredited their participation, casting a disturbing shadow over the whole rebellion.[13] But even in these cases, the attacks – though indefensible – were not so much random or arbitrary as they were racist and misogynist. Even these ill-chosen targets were not randomly singled out, but fell victim to a morally corrupt set of convictions on the part of some rioters about which targets to attack.

Ellwood's definition of rioting will not suffice, because it deflects our attention from the very possibility that a riot can be an act of democratic protest. But neither should we adopt a conception of rioting that glosses over the capacity of rioters to act wrongly and to engage in unsound forms of struggle. A suitable definition of rioting must enable discussion of both justice-motivated rioters who act to defend the community against obvious wrongs by indifferent elites, and the malevolently motivated rioters who carry out anti-Semitic pogroms or other wrongful acts. More broadly, the definition should not prejudge questions of normative soundness by injecting into the word's meaning a moralistic disdain for the riotous mob or a radical's hagiographic celebration of the courageous rioter for justice. The definition should be replaced with a basically neutral description, so that it can be used to make judgments, without embedding unexamined prejudgments in the meaning of the word itself. In this spirit, I propose a competing definition, informed by the insights of the crowd historians, but also receptive to Ellwood's insight that rioters can sometimes act wrongly and in such a way as to terrorize people.

I propose to define the term "riot" to mean *an outbreak of civil defiance, in which a crowd openly, directly, and persistently rejects the authority of the established legal order and its enforcers in the military or the police.*

My definition departs from the public order definitions above in three key respects. First, references to "three persons, or more" in Ellwood's definition, or to "12 or more persons" in the UK's Public Order Act, are here replaced by the notion that a riot is the work of "a crowd." This is less numerically precise (although clearly the numbers are arbitrary in any case), but it makes explicit that riots are a form of collective action. This is presumably implied by Ellwood's suggestion that rioters are "assembled together . . . with a fore-intent and purpose," and by the Public Order Act's reference to being "present together . . . for a common purpose." Strictly speaking, however, a crowd of rioters may not share a common purpose, even though in some recognizable sense they do act in common, as a crowd.

Second, references made in the public order definitions to the creation of fear – the "manifest terror of the people," or the "person of reasonable firmness" led to "fear for his personal safety" – are replaced by a reference to the "outbreak of civil defiance." This distinction draws attention to the status of riots as mass rejections of constituted legal authority. Frightening people may or may not be a typical effect of riots. Certainly some behaviour in some riots is frightening. Moreover, some riots, notably racist pogroms, are specifically designed to frighten. But, by its nature, the riot is a kind of conjunctural repudiation of law and order: a refusal, in practice, to accept the authority of the state, its laws, or its law enforcement officials, for the span of time during which the riot unfolds. Whereas fear is an occasional by-product of many riots, it is not an essential feature of all riots as such. The crowd's defiance of law and order, by contrast, is an essential and inherent feature of rioting.

The final difference between the public order definitions and mine is that I join the historians in treating violence, or harm to persons or property, as a nonessential feature of rioting. It is quite possible to join in a riot and participate fully in it, without acting to harm any person or damage any property. Again, the crucial variable is defiance, not destruction or physical aggression against people.

Taking my definition into account, the question becomes: When, and on what basis, is it sound or admirable to participate in a riot, understood to mean an outbreak of civil disorder, in which a crowd openly, directly, and persistently rejects the authority of the established legal order and its enforcers?

A Typology of Riot Genres

From the point of view of the democratic standard, the most notable feature of rioting is not the physical assaults or property damage they may entail, but the way they may open up opportunities for a distinctive style of civic engagement: the defiance of legal authorities by grievance-motivated crowds. At times, this sort of civic engagement can play an important role in fostering democracy. This is why the Stonewall case is interesting. It typifies the kind of action that the historians' public autonomy conception of rioting aims to highlight. Clearly, however, many riots do nothing of the sort.

Sporting-event hooliganism, for instance, often takes the form of rioting, and some of this rioting may even have a political motive.[14] But in many cases, it simply serves as a vehicle for the expression of drunken, young male, thrill-seeking aggression. In these cases, it contributes nothing whatsoever to public autonomy or democratic politics. In the same way, the rioting behaviour on display in the anti-Semitic pogrom riots in the nineteenth-century Russian Empire had nothing to do with autonomous democracy.[15] In order to see when and on what basis rioting can function as a language of the unheard, and when it cannot, we need to distinguish between different kinds of rioting behaviour. A simple typology of rioting genres can help to disaggregate rioting behaviours, and thereby assist in the task of normative assessment.

Grievance Rioting

For my purposes, the most notable type of rioting is what I call grievance rioting. Grievance rioting defies public order in order to press a grievance. That is, it uses defiance as a type of protest. A classic example would be the Los Angeles Rebellion (or LA Riots). This outbreak of large-scale defiance unfolded over the course of four or five days in late April and early May of 1992. The rebellion was provoked most directly by the acquittal of the Los Angeles police officers accused of using excessive force in the brutal and prolonged beating of an African American man named Rodney King during an arrest. The attack had been captured on video by a nearby amateur photographer – which, in the early 1990s, had not yet become commonplace – and the footage had been seen by millions of people. The police were shown in the video remorselessly beating a defenceless and largely immobile King for several minutes. It was hard to regard the jury's refusal to convict King's attackers as anything other than a racist message that brutal police violence was acceptable, as long as it was directed against African Americans. If the attack on King did not qualify as excessive force, then presumably no amount of force would be excessive. The riots began on the day the acquittals were announced.

The scale of the uprising in LA was vast. In the course of the sustained and complicated confrontation, at least 52 people died, 16,291 were arrested, 2,383 were injured, and approximately 20,000 police and military personnel were deployed.[16] Although the riots have often been depicted in simplified racial terms, as if they were straightforwardly a riot of African Americans indignant about the brutality of white police officers and the racism of the legal system, historian Gerald Horne notes that "a plurality, 36.9 percent, of those arrested were Latino . . . and only 29.9 percent were black."[17] One layer of interracial (and gender) complexity was added by the fact that the King verdict had been preceded by another, seemingly related trial verdict. About five months earlier, a Korean American shopkeeper had been given a suspended sentence and five years of probation for her voluntary manslaughter conviction for shooting a young African American teen, Latasha Harlins, after accusing her of trying to shoplift a container of orange juice.[18]

The complexity of the Los Angeles Rebellion makes it impossible for me to do justice to the full story of what happened and why.[19] But one thing is clear: most of those who joined in this outbreak of civil defiance were clearly grievance motivated. For most, the rioting was directed against the impunity of the LA police, which for decades had targeted racial minorities for abuse, assault, and humiliation, not exceptionally or in the single case of Rodney King, but persistently and routinely. The LA uprising offers a vivid example of a riot event dominated by grievance rioting, but it also underlines the complexity of large-scale riot events and the impossibility of judging a riot as a whole, as if it were a unitary phenomenon.

Acquisitive Rioting

A second type of rioting behaviour, which may occur separately or alongside grievance rioting, is acquisitive or consumer rioting. Acquisitive rioting usually takes the form of crowd-initiated looting of stores. Martin Luther King described acquisitive rioting as "a kind of stormy carnival of free-merchandise distribution."[20] Here we have to be careful. The mere fact that looting occurs does not rule out the possibility that the behaviour could be grievance rioting. One could loot as a means of displaying defiance and protest. King himself points out in his discussion of looting that "property represents the white-power structure, which [rioters] were attacking and trying to destroy," so that there is sometimes an unmistakable "symbolic aspect of the looting for some who took part in it."[21]

Looting should only be considered acquisitive rioting if, without particularly trying to protest anything, rioters attempt vigorously to acquire goods at no cost, seizing the opportunity of a breakdown of civil order to gain access to consumer goods that might otherwise be unaffordable. It may be impossible to tell the difference between two looters, one of whom loots to express defiance and indignation as a grievance rioter, while the other loots to acquire free consumer goods as an acquisitive rioter. Even individual looters could have ambiguous or conflicting motives, or they could be unsure of exactly why they are looting. The UK's London Riots of August 6–10, 2011, began with typical grievance rioting, sparked by the police killing of a young black man, Mark Duggan. In the course of the riot, however, the looting was so extensive that many observers expressed the view that acquisitive rioting had become an important factor in the events. Social theorist Zygmunt Bauman saw the rioters as "defective and disqualified consumers," impelled by "the temptation to have," that is, to consume, and "the spite and grudge aroused by *not* having."[22] Slavoj Žižek took a similar view, describing the rioting as "envy masked as triumphant carnival."[23] Others, including writer Darcus

Howe, called the riot "an insurrection of the masses" and in that sense an outbreak of grievance rioting.[24]

Nevertheless, even though the distinction can be difficult or impossible to draw clearly, there is a difference in principle between these two motives. Rioting to acquire consumer goods is not militancy, so it cannot be democratically sound militancy. But looting as a type of defiance and rebellion may well be a language of the unheard and an expression of civic virtue.

Recreational Rioting

Rioting is recreational when its primary motive is to indulge in exciting or fun types of crowd activity. Here again, it may be difficult to draw distinctions clearly in practice, but the difference between recreational and grievance rioting is important to insist upon.

A good example of recreational rioting occurred in June 2011, in Vancouver. The 2011 Vancouver Stanley Cup Riot, as it is known, erupted after the local pro hockey team lost the National Hockey League championship series. Approximately 150 people were arrested, and about 200 were injured, including at least four who were stabbed.[25] The riot was evidently not sparked or sustained by any desire to protest about a grievance, but simply by the desire to create exhilaration and amusement by means of vandalism and alcohol-fuelled confrontation. After the local team lost the final game in the series, disappointed fans vented their displeasure by throwing empty beer bottles at large-screen TVs set up in Vancouver's downtown. Then a few people began upending portable toilets. Soon, cars were overturned. When the police responded with aggressive force, the hockey fans replied by throwing bottles at them. As the spectacle escalated, fires were started and stores were looted.[26] Few observers mistook this for a grievance riot.[27]

Authoritarian Rioting

A fourth genre is authoritarian rioting. A rioter who tries to exploit a breach of civil order, hoping to seize the opportunity to assert dominance over others by intimidating, attacking, or humiliating them, is engaged in authoritarian rioting. I call it authoritarian because, whereas grievance rioting adopts an oppositional stance toward the forces of order, like the police or the military, the authoritarian rioter shows signs of relishing the chance to impose by force a new order, stepping happily into the posture of the weapon-wielding thug, barking orders at people or beating them, sometimes torturing or even ritually massacring them. One of the most noteworthy examples of authoritarian rioting was the Kristallnacht riot unleashed by the Nazis in 1938 across Germany, in which 91 Jews were killed, many more were beaten or rounded up into concentration camps, and massive destruction was inflicted on homes, businesses, and synagogues.[28]

As the example of Kristallnacht shows, authoritarian rioting can be the animating force for a whole riot. This was also the case in the 1921 Tulsa Race Riot spearheaded by the white supremacist Ku Klux Klan and other racists, which left several dozen African American residents of Tulsa dead and thousands homeless.[29] In other riots, however, authoritarian rioting figures only as one small element in a much larger mix, as in the case of the transport worker who was pulled out of his truck and beaten almost to death by six people during the LA Riots, an abusive attack that had very little in common with the grievance rioting of most uprising participants.[30] In such cases, the democratic standard, notably the common decency requirement built into the accountability principle, strongly rejects any move to blur the distinction between democratic grievance rioting and the opportunistic use of the riot as an occasion to indulge authoritarian revenge fantasies by victimizing vulnerable individuals.

Rioting and Voice

The implications of this differentiation of rioting into multiple genres should be clear. Whether rioting activity – within a larger riot event – is admirable for its contribution to autonomous democracy will depend, first and foremost, on the genre of the rioting. It seems clear that authoritarian rioting, which aims to abuse, dominate, or humiliate vulnerable persons, never complies with the values promoted by the democratic standard. It is also undeniable that recreational and acquisitive rioting are incapable of satisfying the democratic standard of soundness. The reason is not that they are necessarily abusive and vicious, like authoritarian rioting, but that, by definition, they are not forms of protest at all and so cannot be admirable forms of protest. If rioters act in carnivalesque ways, in the context of grievance-motivated civil defiance, then this is not recreational but grievance rioting, as I have defined these terms. And if rioters loot, not simply to gain access to consumer goods, but out of an impulse to lash out against injustice, then this is likewise not acquisitive but grievance rioting.

In short, the only genre of rioting that can be considered, even potentially, as a language of the unheard is grievance rioting. But when, if ever, should we admire it, and why? In this kind of militancy, as in others, the democratic standard frames the question of soundness in terms of public autonomy. Rioting that contributes to public autonomy should comply with the expectations set by the democratic standard.

Critics of rioting usually claim, in a nutshell, that however understandable rioting is in response to intransigent elites and unresponsive systems of power, riots are self-defeating in that their outcome is generally to make things worse. Rioting damages the neighbourhoods of those whose grievances supposedly motivate them; the brief attention that a revolt brings to their grievances is fleeting and quickly dissipates into fruitless commissions of inquiry and empty promises. In other words, contrary to the norm set out by the accountability principle, rioting is insensitive to the common good, because the aggrieved are consistently and therefore predictably made worse off by it.[31]

This is a serious worry. Riots do impose costs on communities, and those costs often fall disproportionately on the least advantaged. It was not the most affluent neighbourhoods, and certainly not large corporations or other elites, that bore the brunt of the LA Riots, for instance. It was mostly small shops and neighbourhood infrastructure that were damaged or destroyed, and many thousands of poor people from South Los Angeles were injured, laid off, or criminally charged in the aftermath.

Even so, in spite of the high cost, important benefits may also have been won by the rioting, even if they are harder to quantify than some of the costs. The benefits I have in mind are captured by the important, if somewhat intangible, concept of voice, upon which my analysis has relied throughout this book. As I mentioned in chapter one, my understanding of voice is informed not only by King's use of it to describe the militant's vocation, but also by economist Albert O. Hirschman's use of it to talk about the dynamics of dissatisfaction and power.[32]

"Voice" is defined by Hirschman as the capacity of participants in a relationship or organization to seek changes in the terms of that participation by expressing their grievances or by communicating proposals for change. He contrasts voice with "exit": the capacity of participants to opt out of the relationship or organization if they find it unsatisfactory. Someone who is merely subject to a legal order, but not one of its members, has two options: to leave or to obey. But someone recognized as a member of that order has the additional option of voicing their grievances and aspirations, expecting to be heard and taken seriously. With membership, one can argue with one's peers, as a co-deliberator in a process of self-governance through discussion and argumentation.

If voice is what elevates the status of people from subjects to members of a legal order, then the voiceless, the unheard, are at least in one important respect excluded from the terms of that relationship. As silenced, ignored, invisible members, as members without voice, they are in a real sense not members at all. Or, at least, they lack one of membership's characteristic advantages. They are, in short, second-class members. In democratic-theoretical terms, grievance rioting recommends itself mainly as a potential remedy for this denial of voice. Grievance rioting is a kind of demand to be heard; it is a refusal to be ignored, expressed as defiance of the authority of the established legal order.

Because they lack voice, the unheard confront in the state and its legal regime not an expression of their own autonomy as members of a self-governing political community, but an alien power that imposes laws from above, which they have no reason to regard as legitimate. But how can the unheard, the voiceless, or the disenfranchised address their lack of voice? Hirschman suggests that the extent of one's capacity to influence a relationship or organization – the extent of one's voice – is partly determined by the availability of exit options. If people have no capacity to opt out of a relationship, then their counterparts in those relationships need not be very concerned about their dissatisfaction. If there is only one cab company in town, the company need not worry very much that poor service will lead to a loss of business. Given the lack of exit options, customers have no way of taking their business elsewhere. By contrast, if there are competitors who are only too happy to pick up any new business that might come their way, there is a much greater incentive for the company to listen carefully to complaints and to satisfy disgruntled customers, in order to retain their patronage. Hirschman concludes that the extent of one's voice in a relationship or organization depends crucially on one's access to viable exit options.

One way to think of riots is as a kind of exit: a temporary withdrawal from attributing authority to the legal order. One cannot exit from the brute power of the enforcement regime backing up the legal order, with its batons, guns, handcuffs, and prisons. But one can exit, or opt out of, the social practice of ascribing authority to it. That is, one can defy it.

It's a simple thought. Readers of Hirschman's book will know that there is a great deal more to be said about the dynamics of exit and voice. But I want only to draw attention to a correlation: other things being equal, the availability of exit options encourages people in power to pay more attention to one's voice, because it creates leverage that one would not have in the absence of an effective exit option. So one response to voicelessness is to create or draw attention to possible exit options.

To be sure, there are other ways, short of rioting, to exit from a legal order in which one has little or no voice. There is emigration, that is, physical exit in the literal sense. There is also the option that Jürgen Habermas calls "civic privatism," the retreat from engagement with public affairs into the privacy of career ambitions, recreational pursuits, and personal relationships.[33] But neither of these modes of exit has a voice-enhancing effect. On the contrary, these options only deepen one's incapacity to effect change within the regime. What about that third mode of exit, rioting – does it have the potential to enhance the voice of the unheard?

Clearly, rioting is not the sort of thing that Hirschman has in mind when he discusses exit. After all, rioters only leave the legal order (by defying its authority) on a short-term basis, for the duration of the riot itself. More importantly, they do not leave the legal order in quite Hirschman's sense, since they are still living within the jurisdiction of the order they reject. So grievance rioting is, on the one hand, a mode of civic participation or engagement, and on the other, a mode of exit from the legal order. It is, one could say, a kind of engaged exit. But what recommends it is precisely what is lacking from emigration and civic privatism: it strengthens the voice of the voiceless. Rioting has a kind of enfranchising effect: by opening up an avenue of exit, and thus threatening the state with a breakdown of its claim to authority, rioting creates a strong incentive to listen to what the unheard have to say.

Certainly, there are often grave costs: burned cars, broken windows, economic disruption, injured and arrested people, almost always falling disproportionately in neighbourhoods in which poor and marginalized people live. And yet, people continue to riot. Is this just irrational, self-defeating behaviour? Or might the voice-enhancing effect of engaged exit create a powerful incentive to rebel, when other avenues for gaining a hearing prove fruitless?

Looking at the history of rioting, especially in cases where the riots are large-scale and substantially destructive, the riot is often quickly followed by an investigation or commission of inquiry tasked with identifying the causes of the riot and proposing recommendations. Of course, appointing a panel of experts to investigate the grievances of some excluded or oppressed group is a far cry from simply empowering them to speak for themselves and to take decisions about how to run their communities directly. Indeed, it is no doubt correct, as David J. Olson said in his pioneering analysis of these inquiries, that "riot commissions are essentially conservative devices by which political executives remove pressure from themselves for meaningful and immediate action by consigning racial problems to study."[34]

Nevertheless, these commissions are a symptom of an important shift. Suddenly, previously intransigent elites and unresponsive institutions take an interest in what the silenced and ignored might be so upset about. The unheard are invited, at last, to speak. The Kerner Commission, for example, was established by the Johnson administration in late July 1967, in response to major rioting in Newark, New Jersey, and Detroit, Michigan, earlier that month. In the commission's famous report, one sees the logic of elite response to exit threats explicitly highlighted:

> The President of the United States established this Commission and directed us to answer three basic questions: What happened? Why did it happen? What can be done to prevent it from happening again? To respond to these questions, we have undertaken a broad range of studies and investigations.... This is our basic conclusion: Our nation is moving toward two societies, one black, one white – separate and unequal.... Discrimination and segregation have long permeated much of American life; they now threaten the future of every American. This deepening racial division is not inevitable. The movement apart can be reversed.... The alternative will require a commitment to national action – compassionate, massive and sustained, backed by the resources of the most powerful and the richest nation on this earth. From every American it will require new attitudes, new understanding, and, above all, new will.

It hardly needs to be said that "massive and sustained" action to address the grievances of poor people in Newark and Detroit was not ultimately forthcoming. Indeed, a 2011 definitive, book-length study by Lindsey Lupo shows in detail "how riot commissions in the United States in the last one hundred years have each submitted the riot violence to a bureaucratic process, thereby 'processing away' the violence into a non-political, non–civil rights oriented event."[35] This leads many observers to dismiss these commissions as merely public relations exercises designed to appease the unheard without actually having to hear their concerns and take them seriously.

I view these dismissals as one-sided. The point is not that very much of anything comes of these commissions, directly. Rather, they signal a shift in the balance of power: a visible indicator that elites and dominant institutions have found it necessary to recalibrate their political strategies, to take into account the threat posed by populations which, before the riots, they thought they could safely ignore. No style of militancy or protest will suddenly, over the course of a day or two, put the people in charge, deposing elites and their systems of power. Instead, one hopes that the ignored will be harder to ignore, that the silenced might begin to find a voice and to push their grievances onto the agenda of public life. Rioting is no final remedy for the problems of the unheard. But it is not to be discounted, either. It is a sometimes-potent tool in the repertoire of political resources at their disposal.

{ Nine }

Armed Struggle

As a rule, books calling for armed struggle against capitalism do not reach the top spot on the Amazon bestseller list. In July 2009, however, *The Coming Insurrection*, authored by the Invisible Committee, proved an exception to this rule. Though anonymous, the Invisible Committee was identified by the French police with a circle of intellectuals and activists associated with the "insurrectionist" journal *Tiqqun*, published in France between 1999 and 2001. Five women and four men within this milieu, including the "alleged ringleader," philosopher Julien Coupat, were arrested in the village of Tarnac, France, in 2008.[1] Dubbed the Tarnac 9, they were accused of sabotaging the rail system in France, although most of the charges were soon dropped due to lack of evidence. If the identity of the authors is in doubt, the Invisible Committee's commitment to a strategy of armed insurrection is not. "There is no such thing as a peaceful insurrection," the book declares. "Weapons are necessary. From a strategic point of view, indirect, asymmetrical action seems the most effective kind, the one best suited to our time: you don't attack an occupying army frontally."[2] There is more to the book than that, certainly. But it is this thought that interests me here: that an armed insurrection, using urban guerrilla tactics, is suited to our time.[3]

The Invisible Committee is by no means innovating when it makes this suggestion. In the decade and a half after 1968, most of the affluent capitalist countries had at least one and sometimes several radical groups experimenting with armed struggle. In France, for instance, there was Action directe; in Italy, the Red Brigades; in Germany, the Red Army Faction; in Quebec, the Front de libération du Québec; and in the United States, the Black Liberation Army. Each of these groups, and others like them, advocated and to a degree carried out some kind of armed struggle.[4]

If the Invisible Committee has anything to add to the tradition of urban guerrilla activism, it is mainly the introduction of a distinctive intellectual rationale for this strategy, drawing eclectically on themes from the heritage of anticapitalist cultural critique: Max Horkheimer and Theodor Adorno's *Dialectic of Enlightenment*, Herbert Marcuse's *One-Dimensional Man*, Paul Goodman's *Growing Up Absurd*, Students for a Democratic Society's *Port Huron Statement*, and above all, Guy Debord's *Society of the Spectacle*.[5] The urban guerrilla groups of the 1970s and 80s relied on earnest moralism and a sometimes self-righteous insistence that "the duty of every revolutionary is to make revolution."[6] By contrast, the Invisible Committee relies on a string of jaded and ultra-intellectual observations on the malaise of contemporary French culture to make its case. Nevertheless, the final pages of *The Coming Insurrection* arrive at a familiar conclusion: "Weapons are necessary."

In this final chapter, I consider armed struggle as a style of militancy, confronting the difficult question: When, if ever, should militants engage in armed force?

Pacifism versus the Common View of Violence

To many, there is no question. The use of armed force to kill or threaten people can never be defended as sound militancy, because recourse to coercion or assault, to say nothing of killing, is the very opposite of democracy. But one theme that I have insisted upon throughout is that it is a mistake to use the violence/nonviolence contrast to draw the line between sound and unsound militancy.

One reason we should reject nonviolence as the crucial criterion is that a rigid repudiation of any and all armed force would lend credibility to the extreme view known as absolute pacifism. As philosopher Andrew

Fiala says, "absolute pacifists . . . argue that all use of violence is unjustified."[7] There are people who regard themselves as pacifists, but not absolute pacifists. For example, Bertrand Russell called himself a "relative pacifist" and Albert Einstein called himself a "dedicated pacifist," and both explicitly contrasted their positions with absolute pacifism, which they rejected. However, both of these men supported Allied participation in the Second World War.[8] To me, it seems odd to suggest that you can be a pacifist and, with no inconsistency, support participation in large-scale wars in which tens of millions of people are killed. I regard this as an absurdly broad definition of pacifism. Accordingly, I reserve the word "pacifism" for opposition to violence in the strict, absolute sense. Less strict views are more plausible, certainly, but the view stops being interesting as a rejection of armed force once it is construed as being consistent with support for massive employments of military violence.

Too often, we overlook the sheer eccentricity of the (absolute) pacifist doctrine. A pacifist, as I use the term, is someone who rejects the use of physical force, even when it could be used to advance urgently important ends or protect against serious harms. Most people reject this view out of hand. As Fiala points out, those who accept it often do so out of religious motives.[9] I see no reason to condemn them for this choice. In the context of spiritual matters, a vow not to kill or harm other beings is akin to other ascetic vows, such as vows of material simplicity, celibacy, or silence. These may be beneficial or worthy in important ways. But it would be a grave error to mistake pacifism for a plausible judgment about our obligations. Most people are no more committed to a norm of absolute pacifism than they are to a norm of celibacy or silence.

To get a clearer picture about the norms that most people are indeed committed to, let's consider a few scenarios. To start with, imagine that someone were to approach you with a baseball bat, with the clear intention, perhaps out of anger, to hit you over the head with great force. You plead with the attacker to lay down the bat, but to no avail. You, meanwhile, also hold a bat. Unsure about what to do, you ask a nearby pacifist for a quick word of advice about how best to respond. The pacifist does not hesitate: “Reject violence,” you are told. “Do not strike the attacker, lest you become the very thing that you oppose!”

Should you take this advice seriously? There seems to be little or no reason to take the pacifist’s advice here. On the contrary, it would not only be understandable, but also entirely acceptable for you to resort to striking the attacker – reluctantly, perhaps, but no less forcefully – to repel this aggression and defend yourself from a serious threat.

In this scenario, self-defence might be seen as the variable that makes the difference. Perhaps, then, even the pacifist could – making a rather remarkable concession – treat self-defence as a special case: the exception that proves the rule. But on reflection, self-defence is not necessarily the crucial factor. Imagine that it is not you that the attacker approaches, but a neighbour. You, however, remain in possession of the bat, and everything else is as before. Again you ask the pacifist, “What should I do? Should I strike the attacker?” This time, you are not asking about self-defence, but about whether or not to intervene in defence of someone else who is under attack. Knowing what you know about the pacifist’s moral convictions, it will not surprise you to receive the reply: “Whatever you do, do not strike the attacker! This is not even a case of self-defence!”

Again, notwithstanding the pacifist’s absolutist disdain for using weapons, it is hard to deny that it is at least morally permissible for you to intervene in defence of your neighbour by swinging your bat at the attacker. You may indeed be morally required to do so. It seems absurd to suppose that you would be acting wrongly if you used the bat, judiciously but forcefully, to repel the attacker and defend your neighbour, even though you do not thereby defend yourself.

Where do these intuitive judgments come from? Can these nonpacifist judgments be defended in a principled way? I believe that when we arrive at these judgments, we rely on a set of widely shared, principled, and highly plausible norms concerning resort to force. I call this set of norms “the common view” of physical force (or violence). I call it the common view because it is very widely accepted, across the political spectrum, and thus embraced even by people who disagree about almost everything else, certainly including controversial protest tactics.

This common view of justified resort to armed force may be expressed in the form of three simple, largely uncontroversial theses:

1. Armed force is a bad thing, to be minimized as far as circumstances allow.
2. Armed force may nevertheless sometimes be justified, or even morally required, if there is no other way of defending oneself or others from the threat of serious injury or death.
3. Finally, even when resort to physical force is justified, it must never be indiscriminate (such as by targeting those who pose no imminent threat) or disproportionate (such as by using more physical force than necessary to repel the danger that justifies the resort to force).

This set of norms is very widely accepted, regardless of one's other political or moral commitments. Those who hold highly unusual views, such as absolute pacifism or amoralism, reject the common view, but I would suggest there are very few such people. (I suspect, for example, that both Einstein and Russell would accept something like the common view.)

Of course, one could object that this claim to near-consensus is misleading. After all, it ignores the fact that people who agree with these three theses may nevertheless be unable to agree about who poses a threat of injury, in some situation, or about what constitutes a proportionate response, and so on. This is no doubt true. The consensus here is about fundamental principles, not fine points of interpretation and application. Above all, there is a widely shared conviction that the absolute pacifist must be wrong. If a pacifist condemns a person for pushing someone down a flight of stairs, using the stairs as a kind of weapon, it may at first seem like a sound judgment. But when we learn that the person thus pushed was rushing up the stairs to attack some children on the second floor, we immediately see that the pacifist has gone astray, and crudely conflates the first thesis, that violence is bad and to be minimized, with the absolute pacifist principle, that violence is always to be rejected. The common view pinpoints what the pacifist has failed to grasp: that physical force may be justified, or even morally required, if there is no other way of defending oneself or others from the threat of serious injury or death, and its use is neither indiscriminate nor disproportionate.

The Common View and Defensive Force

I will use the term "defensive force" to mean the resort to armed force in order to defend oneself or others against attacks. The common view seems committed to allowing armed force if it is defensive in this way, but to prohibiting armed force otherwise.[10]

Some defenders of militancy will immediately recoil at the claim that only the defensive use of armed force is justifiable. This constraint, some may fear, would rule out the idea of armed revolution or rebellion, regardless of the context. Given that most people can at least imagine a scenario in which initiating an armed revolt would be justified, and many people can name actual armed revolutions, slave revolts, or other rebellions that they think were justified, the common view would be deeply questionable, if this were one of its implications. For instance, consider a widely admired armed revolt like the Warsaw Ghetto Uprising of 1943, in which Polish Jews launched a rebellion against occupying German soldiers, in a tragically unsuccessful attempt to halt further deportations to death camps. Given that the Germans had already defeated and occupied Poland, and the actual fighting had ceased, would even this uprising be condemned by the common view's restriction of legitimate armed force to acts that repel ongoing military attacks?

A great deal hinges on this point, so I want to approach it carefully. I will respond to this concern in four steps. First, I show that many radicals have shown a willingness to adopt the common view, including its focus on defensive force. Second, I point out that some defensive force is explicitly revolutionary, notably the defence of revolutionary institutions against counterrevolutionary violence. Third, I argue that the notion of defence can be extended to include the defence of people against systemic violence, so that initiating an armed rebellion against systemic violence could be considered defensive in a broad sense. And finally, I draw on a critical analysis of the so-called responsibility to protect (or R2P) principle to develop a new "right to rebel" (or R2R) principle, which spells out when and on what basis initiating armed rebellion is justified, in terms of the common view. The rest of the chapter will look at different models of armed force, and assess them using the democratic standard.

It is worth noting upfront that the common view has had many important proponents within the militant left. Indeed, some of the most vocal critics of pacifism in recent decades, such as Malcolm X, the Black Panther Party, and others, have assumed as a matter of course not only that violence is to be minimized, as far as circumstances allow, but also that the primary justification for resorting to armed force is that it may sometimes be necessary in order to defend oneself or others from aggression. Despite many years of militant activism, neither Malcolm X nor the Black Panther Party ever carried out an offensive use of weapons, nor did they urge others to do so. Indeed, the Black Panther Party was in its early years called the Black Panther Party for Self-Defense. But this reluctance to embark on the offensive use of armed force was not a symptom of pacifism. It was an expression of a commitment to the common view of armed force: that it is to be minimized, as circumstances allow; that it is sometimes justified, notably when it is necessary to repel aggressors; and that even when it must be used it should not be used indiscriminately or on a scale disproportionate to the threat.

The perception among some that Malcolm X or the Black Panthers were committed to anything other than the common view derives from the fact that, when they talked about self-defence, they meant black people defending themselves against the lawless violence perpetrated or threatened by white police officers and racist vigilantes. The idea that it is acceptable to use force to repel an armed attack by a lawless and violent aggressor is not, as such, controversial. In the context of a racist worldview, however, it becomes shocking once one specifies that the aggressor to be repelled is white and the person or people repelling the aggression are black. Philosophically, however, this double standard is specious and must be discarded by those still in its grip.[11]

I mention these points simply to clarify the issue before us here, and to dispel confusions that distort thinking and debate on these difficult questions of ethics. Above all, we need to discard the false dichotomy according to which we must either embrace armed force regardless of whether it is offensive or defensive, or adopt the absolute pacifist prohibition of all armed force, even when its role is defensive. Both the nature of the questions to be addressed, and the candidates for a plausible answer here, are bound to be more sensitive to the subtleties and ambiguities that complicate these matters in real life.

Moreover, it needs to be pointed out that some specifically revolutionary uses of armed force are clearly permitted, even on the most narrow understanding of what we mean by defensive armed force. For example, the Paris Commune was a radically democratic, community-based system of localized self-rule, established in Paris, France, in 1871. Many revolutionaries, notably Karl Marx, sang its praises at the time, hailing it as a poststatist, egalitarian political community that had embarked on creating a revolutionary democratic socialist order.[12] When the French army, at the close of the Franco-Prussian War, launched an invasion of the city to restore the old order and crush the outpost of public autonomy that Parisians had established there, everyone expected a bloodbath if the army proved victorious. The women and men of the Commune organized a valiant armed defence of the city against the army's aggression.[13] In the end, the makeshift barricades, light arms, and ill-trained militia of the Communards proved incapable of fending off the experienced and well-equipped professional army that attacked and soon crushed the Commune. In addition to the thousands who died in combat, thousands more were murdered summarily or after military show trials. As historian Donny Gluckstein notes in his study of the Commune, "there are no incontrovertible figures for the final count of victims subsequent to the 'victory of law and order.' Estimates range from Du Camp's gross underestimate of 6,500, through Lissagaray's 20,000 to 37,000."[14] Many thousands more were imprisoned or exiled, precisely because they had defended democracy against the army. Certainly, the common view of armed force permits defence against attackers who threaten an impending bloodbath.

But while the Paris example proves that there are cases of revolutionary defensive armed force, consistent with the common view, it remains clear that most of the use or advocacy of armed force for revolutionary ends is rooted in an offensive strategy for using military force to initiate a process of far-reaching social change. The Invisible Committee's call for "asymmetrical" armed attacks is a case in point. So, too, is radical writer and activist Ward Churchill's call for willingness to expand our tactical repertoire into "the realm of 'offensive' military operations (e.g., elimination of critical state facilities, targeting of key individuals within the governmental/corporate apparatus, etc.)."[15] To cite a more classical source, the claim by Marx and Engels in the *Communist Manifesto* that anticapitalists favour "the forcible overthrow of all existing social orders" also seems to point toward the need, under certain conditions, to have recourse to armed force.[16] Does the common view of armed force allow the consideration of such measures, or does it rule them out altogether?

Systemic Violence and the Right to Rebel

Many philosophers and social movement activists would insist that, in addition to violence of the ordinary kind, which consists of direct physical attack, there is also another kind of violence, systemic violence. Systemic violence (a concept we encountered in chapter two) consists of grave harms that victimize vulnerable people in various ways, such as by subjecting them to deep and persistent poverty, poor health, unsafe working conditions, grave human rights violations, racially motivated incarcerations, and substantially reduced life expectancy.[17] These effects are achieved with social structures instead of weapons, but they are not for this reason any less violent. Slavoj Žižek defines this systemic violence as "the often catastrophic consequences of the smooth functioning of our economic and political systems."[18] A line from Woody Guthrie is apt here: "Some will rob you with a six-gun, and some with a fountain pen."[19]

Certainly, many people will regard Žižek's definition as overstretching the word "violence" and forcing it to cover too much ground. Even so, the systemic violence thesis is surely quite plausible, if it is understood (as it should be) not as a claim about what the word "violent" means, but rather as a claim about the moral equivalence of conventionally violent harms, and injuries inflicted by the functioning of social systems and structures. When government policy effectively deprives many people of access to a basic income, when industry restructuring throws thousands out of work, or when people with disabilities are denied access to the resources and services they need to participate fully in social life, these systemic impacts may harm the affected people far more gravely than if they had simply been punched in the face. As such harms start to affect mortality rates and condemn some people to persistent poverty, social exclusion, police violence, a lifetime of impaired earning potential, and so on, the extent of the harm may constitute moral injuries on a scale that matches or even exceeds that of many forms of manifestly violent armed force. This possibility is acknowledged whenever one speaks of a "war on the poor" or a "war on women," and so on.

This thesis about moral equivalence is important, because it licenses the extension of the concept of defensive armed force to a wider range of cases, including cases where force is initiated by rebels in order to put a stop to systemic violence. If the status quo is already violent – if people are always already under attack by unresponsive systems of power – then perhaps striking out against the social structures that institute this systemic violence is acting in a way that is morally equivalent to mounting a military defence against aggression, even if it is the rebels who initiate the combat.

The idea of broadening the notion of defensive force to include cases where combat is initiated to stop ongoing harms, rather than to repel attacks, is not entirely alien to the mainstream discourse on the justifiable use of force. Specifically, many mainstream just war theorists have in recent years adopted the idea that emergency interventions to put a stop to gravely injurious or destructive threats to human security can be justified, even in the absence of an active military threat that needs to be repelled. In other words, they suggest that, in addition to defending against aggression, a further sound reason to initiate a military confrontation is to stop grave harms from continuing. This justification has come to be discussed under the heading of the "responsibility to protect," or R2P. If the established authorities in some jurisdiction are either unwilling or unable to put a stop to ongoing grave harms being inflicted on a group of people within that jurisdiction, then others have at least a right, and perhaps (if they have the means to carry it out, without paying a disastrously high cost) the obligation to forcefully intervene to stop the grave harms from continuing. According to *The Responsibility to Protect*, the report of an international commission studying so-called humanitarian warfare, one of the basic principles of R2P is that "where a population is suffering serious harm . . . and the state in question is unwilling or unable to halt or avert it, the principle of non-intervention yields to the responsibility to protect."[20]

This principle could address the concerns of those who worry that the common view of armed force precludes the possibility of a justifiable revolution. However, there are serious problems with the principle as it now stands. Most fundamentally, R2P directly contradicts a requirement of the democratic standard. The agency principle urges that the most directly affected people be encouraged to take the lead in securing the resolution of their own grievances, but R2P instead authorizes military attacks by foreign powers, justified on supposedly humanitarian grounds. On that basis alone, R2P is incompatible with sound militancy.

But there are other problems, too. The initiators of the R2P standard propose to restrict the "just causes" that would make armed intervention acceptable to only two: "large-scale loss of life" and "large-scale ethnic cleansing."[21] Their intention seems reasonable: they do not want the warmaking to get out of hand, so they limit it to the worst abuses. That is fair enough. Yet, the list of two types of cases seems arbitrary. In particular, why not follow international law scholar Fernando Téson and add "pervasive and serious forms of oppression"?[22]

This second problem, however, is addressed in the more flexible, yet still demanding, variation on the R2P standard offered by consequentialist philosopher Peter Singer:

> [Initiating armed force] is justified when it is a response (with reasonable expectations of success) to acts that kill or inflict serious bodily or mental harm on large numbers of people, or deliberately inflict on them conditions of life calculated to bring about their physical destruction, and when the state nominally in charge is unable or unwilling to stop it.[23]

Can this principle, which is a variant of R2P, serve as a standard for the justification of armed resistance to defend people against systemic violence? Not quite. Singer's formula makes heavy use of phrases like "acts that kill or inflict," "calculated to bring about," and "deliberately inflict." Once one admits the importance of systemic violence, the problem needs to be reframed in terms of the functioning of systems and institutions, as opposed to acts and deliberate calculations. Nevertheless, three elements of his list of criteria seem worth retaining: his reference to "serious bodily or mental harm on large numbers of people," his insistence that armed force should not be undertaken in the absence of "reasonable expectations of success," and his final point about "the state nominally in charge" being "unable or unwilling to stop it." Drawing these three points together, but integrating the notion of systemic violence, the rejected R2P principle can perhaps be reconstructed into a principle of the "right to rebel." The resulting R2R principle would look something like this:

The initiation of armed force can be justified (as defensive in a broad sense) by appeal to the right to rebel, whenever

1. the existing and ongoing level of systemic violence is so great as to impose serious bodily or mental harm on large numbers of people,
2. the use of arms has reasonable prospects of success in ending the systemic violence, and
3. the established regime is either unable or unwilling to intervene forcefully to stop the systemic violence from continuing.

If this complex principle can be applied in ways that encourage the most directly affected to take the lead in securing the resolution of their own grievances, then it should work as a justification of armed rebellion, in contexts where systemic violence is sufficiently injurious and pervasive. The militant R2R principle addresses both the revolutionary's concern that initiation of force to end systemic violence ought not to be ruled out as inherently unjustified, and the just war theorist's concern that armed force not be launched gratuitously or on frivolous grounds. In this right to rebel principle, the notion of just cause is extended beyond repelling overt aggression, but the principle remains faithful to the common view's insistence that justified force should be defensive. Building on the systemic violence concept, we might call it antisystemic defence: defence against grave injuries caused by systemic violence. In this view, the armed militant may be seen as trying to defend the broader public against gravely injurious systems of power.

This analysis suggests that there are two justifications for the use of armed force by justice-seeking militant social movements: first, the straightforwardly defensive use of force, to repel attacks on militants themselves or on others in whose defence militants act; and second, the antisystemically defensive use of force, intended to put an end to systemic violence that the established authorities are unwilling or unable to stop, in keeping with the militant R2R principle.

Some Examples of Armed Militancy

These reflections strongly suggest that armed force can sometimes have a place in the domain of sound democratic militancy. But does that mean that the democratic standard endorses the sort of armed struggle proposed by the insurrectionist Invisible Committee? How does the democratic standard encourage us to think about these matters?

I will lay a basis for answering these questions by examining four well-known groups of armed militants, each of which has explicitly identified itself as an "army": the Irish Citizen Army, the Zapatista Army of National Liberation, the Black Liberation Army, and the Red Army Faction.

Irish Citizen Army

The Irish Citizen Army (ICA) was formed in the course of the famous Dublin Lockout of 1913, an intense struggle that drew in hundreds of firms and tens of thousands of workers, as employers attempted to destroy the militant Irish Transport and General Workers Union (ITGWU).[24] The violence directed against the locked out workers by the Dublin police and the employers' hired thugs reached such heights of intensity (including torture and assassination) that union leaders, notably ITGWU president Jim Larkin, judged that only an armed self-defence militia could adequately protect union members from further beatings and murders. Its primary role was not insurrectionist, but defensive; it was designed mainly to deter attacks on union members during marches and pickets. Larkin explained the rationale at a 1913 mass meeting of ITGWU workers in Dublin. Sean O'Casey, who was secretary of the ICA and later wrote a short book about it, summarizes the speech:

> Labour in its own defense must begin to train itself to act with disciplined courage and with organised concentrated force. . . . It was legitimate and fair for Labour to organise in . . . [this] militant way to preserve their rights and to ensure that if they were attacked they would be able to give a very satisfactory account of themselves. . . . Captain [Jack] White would take charge of the movement, and he trusted that the various Trades Unions would see to it that all their members joined this new army of the people, so that Labour might no longer be defenceless, but might be able to utilise that great physical power which it possessed to prevent their elemental rights from being taken from them.[25]

The Citizen Army initially armed itself with wooden hurleys. In the years after the lockout, however, an effort to consolidate and professionalize the Citizen Army included not only better training and the introduction of uniforms, but also the launch of weapons training. The reorganization of the militia into an armed force proved fateful, for it eventually drew the Citizen Army into a tactical alliance with another armed militia, the

Irish Volunteers, a nationalist-republican force aligned with the Irish Republican Brotherhood.

Together, the Volunteers and the Citizen Army provided the main fighting force for the 1916 Easter Rising armed rebellion in Dublin, which initiated the armed confrontations that were to lead, by 1921, to the partition of Ireland and the formation of the Irish Free State, while maintaining (to this day) the British occupation of six counties in Ulster. The Easter Rising saw a few thousand militia members, mostly from the Irish Volunteers but with a few hundred women and men from the ICA, take control of the general post office and a few other strategically significant buildings around Dublin. They saw themselves as enforcing the Proclamation of an Irish Republic, which they read aloud and posted around Dublin. They then waited for the British army to arrive and attempt to expel them.

Apparently surprised by the willingness of the British to launch major artillery attacks in downtown Dublin, the ICA and the Volunteers proved unable to hold off the British onslaught. They surrendered and over a dozen key organizers were executed, in addition to the hundreds of militia members who had died in combat. Prior to this climactic event in the ICA's history, the Citizen Army had been substantial in size, but certainly not huge. According to O'Casey, the ICA initially had thousands of members, but shrunk into the hundreds once the nationalist Volunteers militia was formed and proved to be better organized.[26] One of the ICA's rules, that each member had to be in a union, must have helped limit its growth. However, in principle, it aspired to grow rapidly and to draw in as many workers as possible, allowing any woman or man in a union to join the militia and receive training in the use of weapons. One of its initial founding principles stated that "the Citizen Army shall be open to all who accept the principle of equal rights and opportunities for the Irish People."[27] Unlike the conspiratorial Republican Brotherhood, with whose Volunteers it collaborated and eventually fused to form the Irish Republican Army (not to be confused with the later "Provisional" IRA), the ICA itself was not a clandestine organization with a secret membership, but an openly organized wing of a militant trade union organization, with a published constitution and publicly declared officials (often themselves elected leaders of mass-membership trade unions).

The Zapatista Army of National Liberation

In our time, Mexico's Zapatistas or EZLN share a number of features with the former Irish Citizen Army. Like the ICA of old, today's EZLN is closely aligned with, and on most matters takes direction from, a system of non-military, mass-membership, social movement organizations.

> The organization of the [nonmilitary wing of the] EZLN, it is important to note, is probably 150,000 people . . . organized into 1,300 communities, grouped together into 29 autonomous municipalities. These are grouped into five public centers or Caracoles. The Caracoles, which are run by Juntas de Buen Bobierno (Assemblies of Good Government), administer regional autonomy. . . . It is the establishment of these good government assemblies and commissions that oversee the clinic system, the preventive health system, and the educational system, teacher training system, the organic coffee collective, the bicycle repair shops, and the medicinal plant collectives that all go into making the Zapatistas autonomous.[28]

The Zapatistas thus operate on two levels, as a smaller armed militia, and – much more importantly and actively – as a large-scale popular movement with mass participation and independent grassroots-democratic structures, outside the control of their military apparatus. And yet, like the Irish Citizen Army, the EZLN militia itself also draws in thousands of active participants. Lastly, after its initial armed intervention to expel the Mexican state from several towns in Indigenous areas of Chiapas in 1994, the activity of the EZLN militia has been almost entirely defensive: protecting the public autonomy of Indigenous communities from the coercive threat posed by the Mexican authorities and by armed paramilitaries hired by regional business elites. In effect, the role of the EZLN is to defend the grassroots governance structures in rural Chiapas from incursions by the Mexican state or other adversaries of the movement. The democratic ideal of public autonomy provides the raison d'être of the militia, since by its nature "Zapatismo is very consciously accountable to the communities that support it, and committed to decision-making through consultation."[29]

The Black Liberation Army

The Black Liberation Army (BLA), in the United States, began as an offshoot from the Black Panther Party (BPP). It was formed in the early 1970s, largely in response to the state's attempt to destroy the Black Panthers. The state's anti-Panther activity took the form of armed attacks, notably the shooting deaths at police hands of Fred Hampton, Mark Clark, and Bobby Hutton, and dirty tricks that disrupted the party's activities by means of the so-called Counter-intelligence Program, or COINTELPRO.[30]

By the end of the 1960s, the Black Panther Party strained to cope with the intense pressure, fuelling a polarization within the group between a majority who hoped to steer the party toward engagement with the official political process (for example, by fielding candidates in mayoral and city council elections), and a minority who wanted to respond to the state's crackdown by shifting toward a clandestine, paramilitary style of organizing. This latter political project found expression in the emerging Black Liberation Army. According to one expert on the BLA's history, "the increased political repression of the Black liberation movement and particularly the BPP convinced many it was time to develop the underground vanguard. In the face of [the] intense counter-insurgency campaign and court cases, many Panthers concluded it was better to struggle from clandestinity than spend years incarcerated."[31]

For over a decade, roughly from 1970 to 1981, the BLA carried out a series of often lethal attacks, mostly targeting police officers (whom they regarded as military targets), but also at times threatening or attacking others, notably armoured car guards and cashiers. This tendency to blur the distinction between combatant targets (as they understood them) and noncombatant targets is, arguably, symptomatic of the distance that separates small, clandestine, urban guerrilla groups from the wider constituency whose grievances motivate the armed group's formation in the first place. Day-to-day contact with and organizing alongside the wider community fosters a greater sensitivity to community standards of acceptable force, whereas prolonged political isolation and underground activism has the opposite effect. More generally, an inevitable side effect of its move underground was that most of the broad public engagement and outreach activities that the Panthers had undertaken, such as their free children's breakfast programs and free healthcare clinics, could not be conducted within the framework of a clandestine armed struggle group. In principle, the BLA aspired to be part of a larger, broader movement, and not just an isolated network of small armed cells, but it was never able to break out of its marginal situation, a reality it seemed almost resigned to in its 1976 public manifesto:

> Because of objective conditions, namely, enemy activity and the relative low degree of unity within the black struggle, we have decided to build the apparatus separate and distinct (organizationally) from all other mass type groups. This is a tactical necessity.... We know from experience that ... many of our actions may very well be tactical actions or [of] a purely military-psychological nature, and because of this clear political support may seem quite difficult. Nonetheless we intend to clarify all acts of revolutionary violence and accept responsibility for these acts.[32]

In other words, they harboured no illusions that their propaganda-of-the-deed activities would be embraced by the broader public (that is, by the wider African American public, or even its politicized segment), and recognized that for the foreseeable future they would remain politically somewhat isolated. Crucially, however, this meant that they accepted the need to surrender their organic ties to community organizing of the type that the Panthers had pioneered, a predicament that seemed tragically self-reinforcing: they would remain politically isolated, as long as they remained underground; but they would have to remain underground, until they were no longer politically isolated.

The Red Army Faction

The Red Army Faction (RAF) in Germany developed along a similar trajectory to the Black Liberation Army, and on a similar timeline. The late-1960s radicalization had led to a polarization within the West German left that replicated the polarization within the Black Liberation movement in the United States. One wing sought to turn the social power of the radicalization into an electoral force for state-brokered reform; a competing wing rejected such reformism in favour of a leap into clandestine armed struggle, emulating on a much smaller scale the perceived successes of Marxism-Leninist guerrilla armies in parts of Africa, Latin America, and Southeast Asia.

The Red Army Faction, the most prominent of a number of groups in the latter camp, emerged in the wake of the armed action that freed Andreas Baader from custody. Baader had been serving a jail term for a politically motivated arson attack. Ulrike Meinhoff, a well-known journalist, arranged with the authorities to meet Baader on the pretext of intending to collaborate with him on research for a book. A small group of Baader's comrades, in co-ordination with Meinhoff, seized the opportunity to free him from police custody. In the course of the action, a librarian in the building was shot by the insurgents and seriously wounded, apparently by mistake.

Forced underground by the subsequent hunt for the culprits, the initial group – numbering in the single digits – announced the Founding of the Red Army in early June 1970.[33] At first, their main armed actions consisted of fundraising bank robberies. Soon, there were a series of shootouts with police attempting to apprehend accused RAF members. In the course of these early months, the group grew to perhaps a few dozen members. Like the BLA, the Red Army Faction found it necessary to grudgingly accept their estrangement from community organizing and broad popular movement activism:

> Our original organizational concept implied a connection between the urban guerrilla and the work at the base. We wanted everyone [in the RAF] to work in the neighborhoods, the factories, and the existing socialist groups, to be influenced by the discussions taking place, to

> have some experience, to learn. It has become clear that that doesn't work. The degree to which the political police can monitor these groups, their meetings, their appointments, and the contents of their discussions is already so extensive that one has to stay away if one wants to escape this surveillance.[34]

In May 1972, the RAF escalated their activities beyond bank robberies, launching a series of bombings that mostly targeted police and military facilities and personnel, but also targeted a judge for a car bomb attack (and inadvertently injured the judge's wife instead).[35] Right-wing media corporation Springer, Inc., was also targeted for a bombing that injured seventeen workers (after warnings to evacuate the building went unheeded). Soon, many members, notably a number of key figures involved in the RAF's founding, including Baader, Meinhoff, Gudrun Ensslin, Jan-Carl Raspe, and Holger Meins, were all imprisoned.

Thus began the second stage in the group's evolution. The focus shifted increasingly toward attacks aimed, directly or indirectly, at liberating RAF members from prison, while also continuing to undertake anti-imperialist and anticapitalist actions. Among the tactics used, three were most characteristic. First, kidnapping and killing members of the ruling class (that is, high-level politicians and business executives, sometimes with a Nazi past), a practice that sometimes led the RAF to kill the bodyguards and chauffeurs of these figures. Second, bombings, kidnappings, and shootings targeting members of the US military stationed in Germany. And finally, in one particularly dramatic episode, the commandeering of the West German Embassy in Sweden, during the course of which certain embassy officials being held hostage were executed to discourage police intervention. The RAF disbanded in 1998.

People's Militias versus Clandestine Cells

As illustrated by this admittedly selective sample of armed struggle activist groups, not all armed struggle is alike.[36] In particular, reflecting on the four groups considered above, two broad styles of armed struggle can readily be distinguished. I call them the people's militia model and the clandestine cell model. Each has had important proponents and practitioners over the course of the past century, but the ICA and the EZLN offer clear illustrations of the people's militia model, and the BLA and RAF, of the clandestine cell model. Extrapolating from these and other examples, some generalizations can be defended.

A people's militia, as I understand the model, has four typical characteristics. First, it operates on a relatively large scale, having at least hundreds and usually thousands (if not tens of thousands) of members. Second, it is nonmilitarist, in the sense that the armed force of the militia is subordinated to higher-level social movement organizations, rather than operating independently. Third, a people's militia, as its name suggests, relies crucially on broad popular support from the wider community outside its ranks, in the absence of which it could not carry out its aims. And finally, it refrains from targeting noncombatants, remaining sensitive to the norm of noncombatant immunity, which is designed to protect innocent bystanders from direct and deliberate attacks.

The large scale of its operations and its close integration with a wider social movement make the boundary between the members of a people's militia and its broader pool of supporters and sympathizers relatively permeable and indistinct. Its members work alongside other social movement activists and participate in all the discussions that constitute the lifeblood of a real popular movement.

The second model, the clandestine cell, can also be analyzed as having four key characteristics, each one contrasting with the features of people's militias. The clandestine cell operates on a very small scale, with its membership often numbering in the single digits, and seldom exceeding a few dozen armed militants. It is typically informed by some version of militarism, suggesting the autonomy of the armed force from any social movement organization. Often, this is accompanied by a claim to function as a kind of leadership or vanguard for the wider struggle.[37] A clandestine cell cannot count on broad popular support, but must accept its own political isolation from the wider community. Finally, the clandestine cell is often either indifferent to or at least suspicious of the notion of noncombatant immunity, preferring instead to discard the distinction between civilian and combatant, usually justifying this stance with an appeal to urgency and a rejection of "clean hands."[38]

Reflecting on these two styles of armed struggle, it is obvious that to ask, Is armed struggle democratically legitimate? is to hopelessly misframe the question. Armed struggle is too vague a designation to serve as the basis for an assessment of its moral or political merits. Instead, the democratic standard must be applied separately to the people's militia project and to the clandestine cell project.

Arguably, many high-profile armed struggle organizations, such as Ireland's (now disarmed) Provisional Irish Republican Army and Palestine's People's Front for the Liberation of Palestine, do not fit neatly into one or the other category, but straddle the divide between them. I do not here try to differentiate the democratic and nondemocratic elements of such hybrid forms. Nevertheless, I hope to shed light indirectly on how one might begin to disentangle the sound (democratic) from the unsound (undemocratic) aspects of such organizations.

Agency and Arms

The democratic standard's agency principle holds that militancy should encourage the most directly affected people to take the lead in securing the resolution of their own grievances.

Applying this principle to evaluating the two models of armed struggle, it is clear that the democratic standard steers toward a people's militia approach. The people's militia is broad-based and accountable to mass-membership social movement organizations, and its members work and struggle in collaboration with justice-seeking social movements. There is no attempt to usurp the agency of the wider movements, or to substitute the bravery and sacrifice of tiny groups of people for the self-activity of thousands or millions. The clandestine cell model, in contrast, has a narrow base of participation. It is structurally unable to collaborate extensively with wider forces, and it often finds itself politically and perhaps even emotionally isolated from the concerns of the wider movements. At times, this isolation is manifested in self-righteous or moralistic disdain for the non-guerrilla left (indicated by their habit of adopting rules prohibiting such attitudes).

These points of divergence are not mere sociological observations. They bear directly on any armed group's claim to democratic legitimacy. Militancy derives its democratic justification from the fact that, under some circumstances, it can challenge the intransigence of elites and the unresponsiveness of systems of power, thereby giving voice to the voiceless, and empowering the public to gain more autonomy. The agency principle points to a way in which militancy can either show due respect for the democratic ideal or fail to do so. If militancy is conducted in a manner that usurps agency from the aggrieved parties, placing leadership and decision-making about the struggle in the hands of a self-appointed counterelite, the effect will be to replicate, within the oppositional movement, the same dynamic of disempowerment and rule by others that constitutes the core of the problem to which militancy is supposed to be a solution. The point is not that the counterelite will be just as bad as the elites that they oppose. This may or may not be the case.[39] Regardless, by installing themselves in the position of self-appointed vanguard or unaccountable elite, they lose their claim on democratic legitimacy. They cannot say that their militancy is a language of the unheard, as long as the unheard remain without voice.

Granting, then, that the agency principle matters for democratic legitimacy, can armed struggle satisfy that principle? In some cases, yes. The Irish Citizen Army and the Zapatistas can be described plausibly as people's militias: they are mass organizations with thousands of members, and they are closely affiliated with, and largely subordinated to, popular organizations with broad and deep roots in the wider community. By developing for the wider movement an armed capacity, these organizations do not displace nonmilitary forms of struggle, nor even make these forms more difficult to carry out (by boosting the odds of successful campaigns of state repression). As long as they steer clear of militarism, or the subordination of the wider movement to the military command structure, there is little danger that they will replace popular struggle with professionalized or semiprofessionalized military struggle. Therefore, they do not usurp popular agency, and it is at least possible that they will satisfy the demands of the agency principle.

Things look different, however, when the same principle is applied to the clandestine cell groups. Their cause may seem just: the need to oppose imperialism or the imperative to end white supremacy are clearly appropriate grounds for recourse to militant action in the public interest. But the clandestine cell model surrenders its claim to soundness when its own practitioners and advocates concede that their mode of struggle makes close engagement with the wider movements, alongside which they had initially hoped to work closely, all but impossible. Tiny groups of individuals – often literally a few, but at most a few dozen – seem ill-equipped to make important decisions about controversial and risky tactics on behalf of the people most affected by those tactical choices, and by the grievances motivating them, when they are structurally cut off from sustained engagement with or accountability to those people.

My point is not that everything the BLA or the RAF ever did was wrong. That is not the case. My point, rather, is that their core political strategy was deeply flawed, in part because it was bound to suffer from a lack of democratic legitimacy. Both groups went down a path that put them tragically in the position of usurping the agency of the people whose grievances they had taken up.

Although it is not a criterion of soundness, an often-reliable indicator that an armed struggle group is on the right track is that they are not normally keen to engage militarily. The Zapatista Army, for instance, does not normally seek out combat situations. Nor did the Irish Citizen Army. They did so occasionally, and famously, but not normally. That is because the struggle is in the first instance a popular struggle, not a military one.

The development of a military capacity may be necessary. The firefighter needs her axe, in case a door can be broken down in no other way. But first she tries the doorknob. The axe is an exceptional tool, to which she may sometimes have to resort, failing the usual methods. For this reason, she keeps it in the truck at all times. In the same way, a militant movement may need to develop a capacity to deter or overpower certain forms of coercive force. Fundamentally, however, a militant social movement is engaged in a political project, not a military one, and the key figures are not soldiers or generals but workers and students, women and people of colour, the excluded and the oppressed, taking action to advance the cause of public autonomy.

Insurrectionism or Self-emancipation?

I began the chapter by noting that the insurrectionist Invisible Committee had proposed a strategy of asymmetrical armed attacks, in a revival of the urban guerrilla strategy popular in the 1970s and 80s. The Invisible Committee apparently had the clandestine cell model in mind, however, which the democratic standard steers one away from adopting. I have made it clear that this is not a pacifist point. It is a democratic point. The clandestine cell model tends to encourage both a usurpation of the agency of the people most affected by the grievances that motivate its adoption, and a tendency to pay less and less attention to the importance of accountability to the democratic values of common decency and the common good, which matter less and less as the clandestine mode of operation intensifies the isolation of militants from the wider social movements out of which they emerge. In other words, it tends to weaken the attachment of militants to the value of public autonomy.

But there is another dimension to this, which is the fact that insurrection, the stated aim of the Invisible Committee, is a profoundly misguided basis for orienting present-day resistance in places like France, Germany, the United States, or Canada – places where the far left remains relatively small and isolated, effectively marginal to the major debates even within oppositional social movements.[40] The focus of the Invisible Committee on such a project, in the absence of any capacity to intervene in broad popular struggles, seems symptomatic of its having run off the rails in some crucial way. The understanding is missing that a rebellion against capitalism cannot be undertaken by tiny grouplets of alienated intellectuals. The autonomy of the people is not only the goal of anticapitalism; it must also be its method.[41]

Anarchists and Marxists have not always agreed on very much.[42] Indeed, Karl Marx and his anarchist contemporary and rival, Mikhail Bakunin, were especially prone to disagree with each other. But there was one key political judgment of which they both became convinced in the late nineteenth century: that "the emancipation of the working class must be the act of workers themselves."[43] This principle of self-emancipation was enshrined in the rules of the organization to which they both belonged, the International, as it was then called, or the First International, as it came to be known.[44]

The principle of self-emancipation, which the International placed at the centre of its politics, first emerged in the mid-nineteenth century as part of a backlash among radicals of that time against earlier forms of socialism that they had come to view as paternalistic and elitist. According to certain earlier forms of radicalism, the "masses" were too ignorant, or too passive and apathetic, to ever liberate themselves, so a special elite of selfless revolutionaries was needed who would achieve social transformation on behalf of working people. Emancipation would be given to the working class as a sort of gift, bestowed on workers from above by an elite of intellectuals and activists. The most forward-looking activists of the time, including Bakunin and Marx, rejected all this and insisted on self-emancipation as a point of principle.[45]

Reading the Invisible Committee's tract, it is hard not to notice that it constitutes a revival, not only of the urban guerrilla strategy of the 1970s, but also of the elitist radicalism to which Marx and Bakunin objected in the late 1800s. Indeed, it is not only the insurrectionists. Far too many of today's self-styled revolutionaries believe that most people are too ignorant and apathetic to liberate themselves, and that they need an elite group of rebels to liberate them from above. They use a slightly different language, but the content of their politics is strikingly similar to the elitist radicalism of the nineteenth century.

Most people are just too apathetic, these activists say, to engage in the struggle for social justice. Most people are sheep, the argument goes, who are wilfully ignorant because of their attachment to consumerism and a self-indulgent lifestyle of hedonism and escapism. The average person is, therefore, part of the problem, not part of the solution. From these analytical starting points, the elitist radicals of today draw the same practical conclusion drawn by their nineteenth-century forerunners: there is no point in trying to mobilize most people, and only people who are true revolutionaries, who reject consumerism and who see through the lies of capitalism and its mass media, can be won over to a strategy of militant struggle, which is needed to take on the system and transform society. The bottom line, for elitist radicalism, is that most members of the general public are not to be seen as a potential force for radical change, to be organized by a painstaking process of movement-building in which they are won over to a transformative, antisystemic political project. Instead, they are best understood as a tool of reactionary politics – bought off by the system, and now so thoroughly incorporated into it, by means of a combination of affluence, consumerism, and mass deception by the media that they are actually part and parcel of the system to be opposed.

When radicals like Marx and Bakunin rejected the politics of elitist radicalism in favour of self-emancipation, they were developing a whole new way of thinking about the dynamics of social change. According to the view they gradually converged toward, changing society is bound up with changing oneself, and people are liberated from oppression or exploitation by mobilizing themselves to struggle on their own behalf. At first, this self-organization, or "self-activity" as Marx called it, might not seem truly revolutionary to other activists, who may think that they know better what the real problems are and what kinds of change are needed. But in the course of such self-activity, the exploited and oppressed not only begin to change the world; they also begin to change themselves. They begin to see the potential power of collective action, to see connections between capitalism and racism or sexism or imperialism that they may not previously have grasped, and they begin to contemplate more and more far-reaching social transformations as they gain deeper insight into the systemic roots of the social problems they hope to remedy through social action.

This process of politicization, sometimes leading to radicalization, may take some time, and different people will draw different political conclusions – some more radical, some more reformist – from their experiences in struggle. But according to advocates of self-emancipation politics, there is no viable alternative to the difficult learning process in which social movements, based on self-organization of exploited and oppressed people, serve as spaces of mediation or bridge-building between millions of people and the transformative agenda of radical politics. Grassroots social movements, in which the unheard claim for themselves a voice, even if it does not seem like a radical or revolutionary voice, are the mediating bridges that make it possible for the ambitious aims for social change embraced by otherwise-isolated radicals to connect to the grievances and aspirations of masses of people with the potential collective capacity to transform society from below.

This is what the Invisible Committee has failed to see. Failing to appreciate the dynamic of self-liberation, they resort to the same elitist, agency-usurping approach to social change that so offended Marx and Bakunin, in which a tiny band of guerrillas or of heroic saboteurs can substitute itself for the missing agency of the millions of people who are not yet revolutionary enough for them.

In the face of this wrong-headed retreat into elitism, the democratic standard steers sharply in the opposite direction. Yes, armed action can sometimes be defensible on democratic grounds, as a means to repel or overpower the coercive force that the enemies of public autonomy sometimes bring to bear against popular empowerment. But the insurrectionist agenda of replacing popular self-activity with a tiny band of heroic urban guerrillas, who will lead the revolution from on high, represents in its own way another threat to public autonomy. One should reject that agenda forcefully, not because the aim of revolution is to be rejected, but because revolution means something different: the self-liberation of autonomous publics.

Acknowledgements

I WISH TO EXPRESS my gratitude to my children, my parents, and my siblings, for their unfailing support and encouragement while I worked on the book. I also want to thank all of the people – too numerous to name individually – who have generously shared with me, in conversations and debates over many years, their opinions and insights about the topics discussed in this book. In particular, I am grateful to all of the activists in London, Ontario, from whom I have learned so much since moving here over a decade ago. I want to thank Tony Weis, from whose wisdom, insights, and kind encouragement I benefited throughout the writing and publication process. Thanks also to Toban Black for several long discussions about the book's key themes, which helped me to clarify my argument; and to David McNally for his helpful advice to me at a critical juncture. I remain very grateful to my former teacher, Ian Hacking, whose approach to the practice of philosophy continues to inspire me. I also want to thank the students and professors who listened, raised questions, and offered feedback on the arguments of the book during a talk I gave in the Department of Philosophy at Huron University College, in early 2013. Thanks to Taylor & Francis, publishers of *Peace Review: A Journal of Social Justice*, for granting permission to reuse in this book parts of my article, "The Militant Protester as Model Citizen." Finally, I am very grateful to Amanda Crocker, Tilman Lewis, and everyone at Between the Lines, for their insights, enthusiasm, and expertise.

Notes

Introduction: Militancy as a Civic Virtue

1 Martin Luther King, Jr., "Speech at Ohio Northern University," January 11, 1968, www.onu.edu.
2 Martin Luther King, Jr., "I Have a Dream," in James Melvin Washington, ed., *I Have a Dream: Writings and Speeches That Changed the World* (San Francisco: Harper San Francisco, 1992), 103. He uses the phrase "magnificent new militancy" in his "Speech at the Great March on Detroit," June 23, 1963, http://mlk-kpp01.stanford.edu. For an overview of King's view of militancy as I understand it, see Stephen D'Arcy, "What Do We Mean by 'Militancy'? Learning from King's Thinking on Militant Protest," ZNet, May 11, 2011, www.zcommunications.org.
3 Martin Luther King, Jr., "Black Power Defined," in Washington, ed., *I Have a Dream*, 160.
4 Martin Luther King, Jr., "Letter from a Birmingham Jail," in Washington, ed., *I Have a Dream*, 91.
5 Peter Gelderloos has argued that "a struggle, to challenge the foundations of this system, must be antidemocratic." Gelderloos, "Reflections for the US Occupy Movement," October 2011, http://libcom.org.
6 The term "deliberative democracy" was introduced into democratic theory by Joseph Bessette, in "Deliberative Democracy: The Majority Principle in Republican Government," in R.A. Goldwin and W.A. Schambra, eds., *How Democratic Is the Constitution?* (Washington, DC: AEI for Public Policy Research, 1980). But it did not emerge as the leading normative theory of democracy in English-language political philosophy until sometime in the 1990s. Arguably, the deliberative turn in democratic theory dates from around 1996, the year in which the two most influential statements of the theory were published in English, viz., Jürgen Habermas, *Between Facts and Norms: Contributions to a Discourse Theory of Law and Democracy* (Cambridge, MA: MIT Press, 1996), and Amy Gutmann and Dennis Thompson, *Democracy and Disagreement* (Cambridge, MA: Belknap Press, 1996), along with an anthology edited by Seyla Benhabib, *Democracy and Difference: Contesting the Boundaries of the Political* (Princeton, NJ: Princeton University Press, 1996), followed by further anthologies in each of the next three years; see James Bohman and William Rehg, eds., *Deliberative Democracy: Essays on Reason and Politics*

(Cambridge, MA: MIT Press, 1997); Jon Elster, ed., *Deliberative Democracy* (Cambridge: Cambridge University Press, 1998); and Stephen Macedo, ed., *Deliberative Politics* (Oxford: Oxford University Press, 1999). For a look at deliberative democratic theory in the context of contemporary democratic theory more broadly, see Ian Shapiro, *The State of Democratic Theory* (Princeton, NJ: Princeton University Press, 2003).

7 Stephen D'Arcy, "The Militant Protester as Model Citizen," *Peace Review: A Journal of Social Justice*, 20, 292–99.

One: The Militant's Vocation

1 Aaron Bobrow-Strain, *Intimate Enemies: Landowners, Power, and Violence in Chiapas* (Durham: Duke University Press, 2007), 4.

2 Jürgen Habermas, *The Crisis of the European Union: A Response* (Cambridge: Polity Press, 2012), 31.

3 Andrew Jacobs, "Farmers in China's South Riot over Seizure of Land," *New York Times*, September 23, 2011.

4 Duncan Meisel, "Case Study: Wisconsin Capitol Occupation," Beautiful Trouble, http://beautifultrouble.org

5 "Anti-Posco Stir: Women Protesters Threaten to Strip," ZeeNews.com, March 8, 2013, http://zeenews.india.com. See also Ashis Senapati, "Anti-Posco Villagers Vow to Oppose Plant," *The Times of India*, March 6, 2013.

6 Martin Luther King, Jr., "MIA Mass Meeting at Holt Street Baptist Church," December 5, 1955, in Clayborne Carson, et al., eds., *The Papers of Martin Luther King, Jr., Volume 3: Birth of a New Age* (Berkeley: University of California Press, 1997), 79.

7 Kurt Andersen, "The Protester," *Time*, December 14, 2011.

8 Mona El-Naggar, "Former Tunisian Leader Faces Legal Charges," *New York Times*, April 14, 2011.

9 Jack Shenker, "Cairo's Biggest Protest Yet Demands Mubarak's Immediate Departure," *The Guardian*, February 5, 2011, www.guardian.co.uk.

10 David Kirkpatrick, "Egypt Erupts in Jubilation as Mubarak Steps Down," *New York Times*, February 11, 2011.

11 "Europe's Most Earnest Protesters," *The Economist*, print edition, July 14, 2011.

12 On the three features of the Occupy model, see Stephen D'Arcy, "'The Political Form at Last Discovered?': Anti-Capitalist Transition from the Paris Commune to the Occupy Movement," paper presented to the Toronto Historical Materialism Conference, York University, May 12, 2012.

13 Tony Clarke, "The Tar Sands and Civil Disobedience," *Toronto Star*, September 25, 2011.

14 Richard Seymour, "Quebec's Students Provide a Lesson in Protest Politics," *The Guardian*, September 7, 2012.

15 On the role of the assemblies, see David Camfield, "Quebec's 'Red Square' Movement: The Story So Far," August 5, 2012, http://newsocialist.org.

16 See the statement "Popular Autonomous Neighbourhood Assemblies: Declaration of Sup-

port for Student Strike," August 4, 2012, http://translatingtheprintempserable.tumblr.com.

17 See John Holloway and Eloina Pelaez, eds., *Zapatista: Reinventing Revolution in Mexico* (London: Pluto Press, 1998).

18 See "South Korea Union Chiefs Increase Strike Militancy," *New York Times*, January 6, 1997. See also "Protesters, Police Clash in S. Korean General Strike," *Chicago Sun-Times*, January 16, 1997.

19 "1995: The French Pensions Strikes," LibCom.org, April 12, 2007, http://libcom.org.

20 See Lesley J. Wood, *Direct Action, Deliberation, and Diffusion: Collective Action after the WTO Protests in Seattle* (Cambridge: Cambridge University Press, 2012).

21 For a detailed, systematic study of the "diffusion" of lessons from Seattle, with specific reference to parts of the activist left in Toronto and New York, see Wood, *Direct Action, Deliberation, and Diffusion*.

22 Martin Luther King, Jr., "A Time to Break Silence," in Washington, ed., *I Have a Dream*, 144.

23 Martin Luther King, Jr., "Conscience for Change," 1967, in John Kenneth Galbraith, et al., *The Lost Massey Lectures* (Toronto: House of Anansi Press, 2007), 175.

24 Albert O. Hirschman, *Exit, Voice, and Loyalty: Responses to Decline in Firms, Organizations, and States* (Cambridge, MA: Harvard University Press, 1970).

25 Ibid., 15–17.

26 Karl Marx, "The Civil War in France," 1871, in R.C. Tucker, ed., *The Marx-Engels Reader*, 2nd ed. (New York: Norton, 1978).

27 Karl Marx, *Ethnological Notebooks of Karl Marx* (Assen: Van Gorcum, 1972), 150.

28 On Marx's understanding of the Haudenosaunee political process, see Franklin Rosemont, "Karl Marx and the Iroquois," http://libcom.org. On the parallels between Haudenosaunee horizontalism and other contemporary models of horizontal democracy, see also David Graeber, *The Democracy Project: A History, A Crisis, A Movement* (New York: Spiegel and Grau, 2013), 180–83. Also relevant is D.A. Grinde and B.E. Johansen, *Exemplar of Liberty: Native America and the Evolution of Democracy* (Los Angeles: American Indian Studies Center, 1991); and Stephen Arthur, "'Where License Reigns with All Impunity': An Anarchist Study of the Rotinonshón:ni Polity," http://nefac.net.

29 Chalmers Johnson, *Revolutionary Change* (Stanford: Stanford University Press, 1982), 97–100.

30 King, "I Have a Dream," 103.

31 Martin Luther King, Jr., "Address at the Freedom Rally in Cobo Hall," in Clayborne Carson and Kris Shephard, eds., *A Call to Conscience: The Landmark Speeches of Dr. Martin Luther King, Jr.* (Atlanta: IPM, 2001), 68.

32 King, "I Have a Dream," 103.

33 King, "Letter from a Birmingham Jail," 87.

34 Ibid., 86.

35 King, "I Have a Dream," 105.

36 Chris Carlsson and Francesca Manning, "Nowtopia: Strategic Exodus?," *Antipode* 42,4 (August 2010).

37 Joyce A. Hanson, *Rosa Parks: A Biography* (Santa Barbara, CA: Greenwood, 2011), 37.

38 The four styles that I highlight here are all mentioned by King, but he uses slightly different terminology. He calls them, respectively, "defiance," "direct action," "violence against things," and "violence against persons." The latter two labels appear in "Conscience for Change."

39 Rosa Luxemburg, "Mass Strike, Party, and Trade Unions," in Dick Howard, ed., *Selected Political Writings of Rosa Luxemburg* (New York: Monthly Review Press, 1971), 223–70.

40 See Huey P. Newton, *Revolutionary Suicide* (New York: Penguin, 2009), 55–59. See also the Black Panther statement "In Defense of Self-Defense: Executive Mandate Number One," in Philip S. Foner, ed., *The Black Panthers Speak* (New York: Da Capo Press, 1995), 40–41.

41 One of the participants in the beating did use a brick, which could be seen as weapon in this context. See John Rogers and Amy Taxin, "Recalling LA Riots, 20 Years Later," *Newsday*, April 28, 2012, www.newsday.com.

42 See chapter 6 of Martin Luther King, Jr., *Stride toward Freedom: The Montgomery Story* (Boston: Beacon, 2010), where Gandhi's philosophy of resistance is singled out as "practically sound."

Two: The Liberal Objection

1 King, "Letter from a Birmingham Jail," 91.

2 Ibid.

3 For a classical radical defence of assembly democracy as a form of popular self-rule, see the essay "Every Cook Can Govern," 1956, in C.L.R. James, *A New Notion: Two Works by C.L.R. James*, ed. Joel Ignatiev (Oakland: PM Press, 2010).

4 John S. Dryzek, *Deliberative Democracy and Beyond: Liberals, Critics, Contestations* (Oxford: Oxford University Press, 2000), v.

5 For an example of an early attack on the influence of money on politics by pioneering deliberative democrats, see Joshua Cohen and Joel Rogers, *On Democracy* (New York: Penguin Books, 1983), especially the opening chapter. The theme goes back even further in the prehistory of the deliberative turn, in the early work of Jürgen Habermas, *Legitimation Crisis* (Boston: Beacon Press, 1975).

6 Seyla Benhabib, "Toward a Deliberative Model of Democratic Legitimacy," in Benhabib, ed., *Democracy and Difference*, 68.

7 See Edward S. Herman and Noam Chomsky, *Manufacturing Consent: The Political Economy of the Mass Media* (New York: Pantheon Books, 1988).

8 Paul Weithman, "Deliberative Character," *Journal of Political Philosophy* 13,3 (September 2005), 263–83.

9 Amy Gutmann and Dennis Thompson, *Democracy and Disagreement* (Cambridge: Harvard University Press, 1996), 79.

10 Leon Trotsky, John Dewey, and George Novack, *Their Morals and Ours: Marxist versus Liberal Views on Morality* (New York: Pathfinder, 1971; originally 1938); Leon Trotsky, *Ter-*

rorism and Communism: A Reply to Karl Kautsky, with a foreword by Slavoj Žižek (London: Verso, 2007; originally 1920).

11 Trotsky, *Their Morals and Ours*, 48.

12 Ibid., 56–57.

13 Friedrich Engels, *The Condition of the Working Class in England*, quoted in Peter Singer, *Practical Ethics*, 2nd ed. (Cambridge: Cambridge University Press, 1993), 308–09.

14 Slavoj Žižek, *Violence: Six Sideways Reflections* (New York: Picador 2008), 1. I return to Žižek and the problem of systemic violence in chapter 9.

15 Malcolm X, *By Any Means Necessary* (New York: Pathfinder Press, 1992).

16 Bernard Williams and J.J.C. Smart, *Utilitarianism: For and Against* (Cambridge: Cambridge University Press, 1973), 116–17.

17 Peter Gelderloos, *How Nonviolence Protects the State* (Cambridge, MA: South End Press, 2007), 3.

18 David Graeber, "Concerning the Violent Peace-Police: An Open Letter to Chris Hedges," *n+1*, February 9, 2012, http://nplusonemag.com.

19 Aric McBay, Lierre Keith, and Derrick Jensen, *Deep Green Resistance: Strategy to Save the Planet* (New York: Seven Stories, 2011), 240–41.

20 The principles are widely available on the internet, for example, here: http://midatlanticua.wordpress.com.

21 See Anna Feigenbaum, "Death of a Dichotomy: Tactical Diversity and the Politics of Post-Violence," *Upping the Anti: A Journal of Theory and Action*, 5 (2007), 189–97.

22 "A16 Revolutionary Anti-Capitalist Bloc," April 16, 2000, http://nefac.net.

23 Pittsburgh G20 Resistance Project, et al., "Pittsburgh Principles," 2009, http://pittsburghendthewar.org.

24 Toronto Community Mobilization Network, "Solidarity and Respect" statement, http://g20.torontomobilize.org.

25 The phrase originates in the US Declaration of Independence, drafted by Thomas Jefferson in 1776, although I have replaced his "mankind" with "humankind." More recently, however, it has been taken up by the American social-democratic political philosopher Michael Walzer, in his book *Spheres of Justice: A Defense of Pluralism and Equality* (New York: Basic Books, 1983), 320, where he describes it as "a respect for the understandings" that people "share with their fellow citizens."

Three: The Democratic Standard

1 Books about the land defence include Geoffrey York and Loreen Pindera, *People of the Pines: The Warriors and the Legacy of Oka* (Toronto: Little, Brown, and Co., 1991); Kiera L. Ladner and Leanne Simpson, eds., *This Is an Honour Song: Twenty Years since the Blockades* (Winnipeg: Arbeiter Ring, 2010); Harry Swain, *Oka: A Political Crisis and Its Legacy* (Vancouver: Douglas & McIntyre, 2010); John Ciaccia, *The Oka Crisis: A Mirror of the Soul* (Dorval: Maren Publications, 2000); Amelia Kalant, *National Identity and the Conflict at Oka: Native Belonging and Myths of Postcolonial Nationhood in Canada* (London: Routledge, 2004); Craig MacLaine and Michael S. Baxendale, *This Land Is Our Land: The Mo-*

hawk Revolt at Oka (Montreal: Optimum Publishing International, 1991). Documentary films on the subject include Alanis Obomsawin, dir., *Kanehsatake: 270 Years of Resistance* (NFB, 1993); Alanis Obomsawin, dir., *Rocks at Whiskey Trench* (NFB, 2000); Alanis Obomsawin, dir., *My Name Is Kahentiiosta* (NFB, 1995); Alec Macleod, dir., *Acts of Defiance* (NFB, 1993); Christine Welsh, dir., *Keepers of the Fire* (NFB, 1994); Catherine Bainbridge and Albert Nerenberg, dir., *Okanada: Behind the Lines at Oka* (Maximage, 1991).

2 McBay, Keith, and Jensen, *Deep Green Resistance*, 265. For their views on the use of armed force, see 269–72. In a nutshell, they endorse a defensive role for armed force, including armed assaults "to reduce the capacity of those in power to do further violence" (271).

3 Ibid., 267.

4 Peter Gelderloos, *Anarchy Works* (San Francisco: Ardent Press, 2010). For his views on armed struggle, see Gelderloos, *How Nonviolence Protects the State.*

5 Taiaiake Alfred, *Wasáse: Indigenous Pathways of Action and Freedom* (Toronto: University of Toronto Press, 2009), 65.

6 Taiaiake Alfred, "Then and Now, For the Land," *Socialist Studies* 6,1 (Spring 2010), 95.

7 George Lakey, "How to Develop Peace Teams: The Light Bulb Theory," Training for Change, www.trainingforchange.org.

8 Although I consulted several sources, for the most part I draw my account of the events from two main sources: Obomsawin's NFB documentary, *Kanehsatake,* and the book by York and Pindera, *People of the Pines.*

9 Quoted in York and Pindera, *People of the Pines,* 78.

10 York and Pindera, *People of the Pines,* 32.

11 According a Canadian Broadcasting Corporation report on the twentieth anniversary of the events, as of 2010 there were "still more than 3,000 aboriginal land claims outstanding – including the one launched by the Mohawk of Kanesatake [Kanehsatà:ke]." CBC News, "Oka Crisis Legacy Questioned," July 11, 2010, www.cbc.ca.

12 For a series of recent reflections on the nature, implications, and impact of the land defence and related events, see Ladner and Simpson, eds., *This Is an Honour Song.*

13 For example, McBay, Keith, and Jensen, *Deep Green Resistance,* 272, criticizes, albeit in mild tones, the Red Army Faction for choosing targets without any apparent concern for whether or not their actions were "effective ways to reduce the state's capacity for violence."

14 Ann Hansen, "Armed Struggle, Guerilla Warfare, and the Social Movement Influences on 'Direct Action,'" in Steven Best and A.J. Nocella II, eds., *Igniting a Revolution: Voices in Defense of the Earth* (Oakland: AK Press, 2006), 342.

15 Joel Bakan, *The Corporation: The Pathological Pursuit of Profit and Power* (Toronto: Penguin, 2003).

16 Jürgen Habermas, *Between Facts and Norms* (Boston: MIT Press, 1998), 306.

Four: Civil Disobedience

1 See John Rawls, *A Theory of Justice* (Cambridge, MA: Belknap Press, 1971), 363–68; Ronald Dworkin, "Civil Disobedience and Nuclear Protest," in Dworkin, *A Matter of Principle* (Cambridge, MA: Harvard University Press, 1985), 104–16; Jürgen Habermas, "Civil

Disobedience: Litmus Test for the Democratic Constitutional State," *Berkeley Journal of Sociology*, 30 (1985), 95–116.

2 King, "Letter from a Birmingham Jail," 90.

3 Marx, "The Civil War in France."

4 Michael J. Nojeim, *Gandhi and King: The Power of Nonviolent Resistance* (Westport: Praeger, 2004), 142–43.

5 Peter Ackerman and Jack DuVall, *A Force More Powerful: A Century of Nonviolent Conflict* (New York: St. Martin's Press, 2000), 88.

6 Ibid., 91.

7 Ibid.

8 Gianni Sofri, *Gandhi and India* (New York: Interlink Books, 1999), 101–2.

9 Nojeim, *Gandhi and King*, 146.

10 John Rawls, *A Theory of Justice* (Cambridge, MA: Belknap Press, 1971), 366.

11 Details are recounted in the letter to university president Amit Chakma from the Canadian Civil Liberties Association, dated April 17, 2012, http://ccla.org.

12 See my opinion piece on the ban, Stephen D'Arcy, "Banning Protesters an Attack on Democracy," *London Free Press*, April 14, 2012. See also the letter to the university president, signed by several faculty members, condemning the ban, David Heap, et al., "Open Letter to President Chakma," *Western News*, April 26, 2012.

13 Dale Carruthers, "Western Blasted for Ban," *London Free Press*, April 17, 2012, www.lfpress.com.

14 Suzanne Goldenberg, "Tim DeChristopher Supporters Issue Oil Protest 'Call to Action,'" *The Guardian*, July 27, 2011.

15 Herbert J. Storing, "The Case against Civil Disobedience," in Hugo Bedau, ed., *Civil Disobedience in Focus* (London: Routledge, 1991), 93.

16 Matthew R. Hall, "Guilty but Civilly Disobedient: Reconciling Civil Disobedience and the Rule of Law," *Cardozo Law Review* 28,5 (April 2007), 2106.

17 In a different context, discussing "welfare fraud" rather than protest, I critique the claim that there is an obligation to obey the law in Stephen D'Arcy, "Is There Ever an Obligation to Commit Welfare Fraud?," *Journal of Value Inquiry* 42 (2008), 377–83.

18 Norman Kretzmann, "*Lex Iniusta Non est Lex*: Laws on Trial in Aquinas' Court of Conscience," *American Journal of Jurisprudence* 99 (1988), 99–122.

19 Plato, *The Laws*, Book IV, 715B.

20 See Christina Fink, "The Moment of the Monks: Burma, 2007," in Adam Roberts and Timothy Garton Ash, eds., *Civil Resistance and Power Politics: The Experience of Non-violent Action from Gandhi to the Present* (Oxford: Oxford University Press, 2009).

21 Gandhi, quoted in Vinit Haksar, "The Right to Civil Disobedience," *Osgoode Hall Law Journal* 41,2/3 (2003), 409.

22 Accusations of lawless police violence during the Quebec student strike are documented in a detailed, 48-page report, *Répression, discrimination et grève étudiante: analyse et témoignages* [Repression, Discrimination and the Student Strike: Analysis and Testimony], published jointly by the Ligue des droits et libertés; the Association des juristes pro-

gressistes; and the Association pour une solidarité syndicale étudiante (April 2013), www.fspd.uqam.ca. For a concise review of the report in English, see Judith Lachapelle, "Mistrust of police and justice has increased" (April 29, 2013), http://translatingtheprintempserable.tumblr.com.

23 Bernard Lafayette, quoted in Ackerman and DuVall, *A Force More Powerful: A Century of Non-violent Conflict* (New York: Palgrave, 2000), 322.

24 Mohandas Gandhi, "Some Rules of Satyagraha," *Non-violent Resistance (Satyagraha)* (New York: Schocken Books, 1961), 79.

25 Martin Luther King, Jr., "Address at Public Meeting of the Southern Christian Ministers Conference of Mississippi," September 23, 1959, in Clayborne Carson, et al., eds., *The Papers of Martin Luther King, Jr., Volume V: Threshold of a New Decade* (Berkeley: University of California Press, 2007), 284.

26 Martin Luther King, Jr., *The Autobiography of Martin Luther King, Jr.*, ed. Clayborne Carson (New York: Warner Books, 1998), 169.

Five: Disruptive Direct Action

1 The expression "direct action" is used in different ways by different people. Martin Luther King used this phrase to describe his own version of classical civil disobedience. Others use the phrase to refer to disruption or to armed struggle. For my purposes, I try to use the expression only when referring to "disruptive direct action," to make it clear that I have disruption in mind, and not classical civil disobedience or armed struggle.

2 Erica Chenoweth and Maria J. Stephan, *Why Civil Resistance Works: The Strategic Logic of Nonviolent Conflict* (New York: Columbia University Press, 2011).

3 Frances Fox Piven, *Challenging Authority: How Ordinary People Change America* (New York: Rowan and Littlefield, 2006), 21.

4 Ibid., 20.

5 According to reports from CNN and other news outlets, the past decade has seen sex strikes carried out in Liberia (2003), Colombia (2006, 2011), Kenya (2008), the Philippines (2011), and Togo (2012). See Frida Ghitis, "A Nation's Sex Strike for Democracy," CNN, August 29, 2012, www.cnn.com; see also Palash Ghosh, "Modern-Day Lysistrata: Togo Women Call for 'Sex Strike' to Force President to Resign," *International Business Times*, August 27, 2012, www.ibtimes.com.

6 See "Idle No More in Toronto: Round Dance Mob Shuts Down Dundas Square," *Rabble.ca*, December 22, 2012, http://rabble.ca.

7 Jeremy Brecher, *Strike!* rev. ed. (Boston: South End Press, 1997), 97–98.

8 Ibid., 232.

9 Ibid., 217.

10 Ibid., 229–30.

11 Adam Fortunate Eagle, *Alcatraz! Alcatraz! The Indian Occupation of 1969–71* (Berkeley: Heyday Books, 1992), 43.

12 Ibid., 14.

13 Ibid., 40.

14 Indians of All Tribes, "Proclamation," in Alvin M. Josephy, Jr., *Red Power: The American Indians' Fight for Freedom*, 2nd ed. (Lincoln: University of Nebraska Press, 1999), 42.
15 Ibid., 41.
16 Fortunate Eagle, *Alcatraz! Alcatraz!*, 88–90.
17 Ibid., 150.
18 Duane Champagne, Tory Johnson, and Joane Nagel, *American Indian Activism: Alcatraz to the Longest Walk* (Urbana: University of Illinois Press, 1997), 32.
19 Robin Morgan, "No More Miss America," August 22, 1968, reprinted in Robin Morgan, ed., *Sisterhood Is Powerful: An Anthology of Writings from the Women's Liberation Movement* (NY: Random House, 1970), 521–24.
20 Carol Hanisch, "What Can Be Learned – A Critique of the Miss America Protest," November 1968, reprinted in Leslie B. Tanner, ed., *Voices from Women's Liberation* (New York: Signet, 1970), 132–36.
21 My account of the day's events relies mainly on the descriptions offered by Jo Freeman, "No More Miss America! (1968–69)," http://jofreeman.com; and Hanisch, "What Can Be Learned."
22 Barry Miles, *Hippie* (London: Sterling, 2005), 16.
23 Ronald Dworkin, "Civil Disobedience and Nuclear Protest," in *A Matter of Principle* (Cambridge, MA: Harvard University Press), 111.
24 The point is developed in chapter 1.

Six: Sabotage

1 Office of Strategic Services, *Simple Sabotage Field Manual* (Washington, DC: Strategic Services, 1944), 2, 3.
2 Ibid., 26.
3 Ibid., 23.
4 Ibid., 8.
5 Eric Hobsbawm, "The Machine Breakers," *Past and Present* 1,1 (1952), 58. Hobsbawm encourages us to place English Luddism in the wider context of tactical "machine-breaking" as one of form of "collective bargaining by riot" (59) in early English working-class history.
6 Book of Judges 9:45. Some interpret the biblical reference to "sowing with salt" as metaphorical or ritual, rather than as a description of the literal sabotage of crops. See R.T. Ridley, "To Be Taken with a Pinch of Salt: The Destruction of Carthage," *Classical Philology* 81,2 (April 1986), 140–46. Even so, it seems likely that such a ritual curse would probably derive its meaning from the prior existence of salting soil as a sabotage technique.
7 Book of Judges 15:4–5.
8 Eric Timm, "Countersabotage: A Counterintelligence Function," *Studies in Intelligence* (Spring 1963), 68.
9 CrimethInc. Ex-workers' Collective, *Recipes for Disaster: An Anarchist Cookbook* (Olympia: CrimethInc. Ex-workers' Collective, 2005), 437.

10 See the Anti-Drug Abuse Act of 1988, H.R.5210, Title VI, Subtitle H. This provision "amends the Federal criminal code to impose criminal penalties on persons who place hazardous or injurious devices on Federal lands with reckless disregard of the risk to another person or with the intent . . . to obstruct the harvesting of timber," http://thomas.loc.gov.

11 Dave Foreman and Bill Haywood, eds., *EcoDefense: A Field Guide to Monkeywrenching*, 3rd ed. (Chico, CA: Abbzug Press, 1993), 19.

12 Judi Bari, *Timber Wars* (Monroe, ME: Common Courage Press, 1994), 279–80.

13 Ibid., 267.

14 Quoted in ibid., 268.

15 Cf. Best and Nocella, eds., *Igniting a Revolution.*

16 The starting date is given in André Moncourt and J. Smith, eds., *The Red Army Faction, A Documentary History, Vol. 1: Projectiles for the People* (Kersplebedeb Publishing and PM Press, 2009), 438. The end date is given in Harriet Torry, "Germany's Once-Violent Feminist Adopts Quiet Life," *Women's eNews*, August 13, 2007, http://womensenews.org.

17 Rote Zora, "Interview with Rote Zora," in Dark Star [Collective], eds., *Quiet Rumours: An Anarcha-Feminist Reader* (San Francisco: AK Press, 2002), 105.

18 As David Gilbert (formerly a key figure in the Weather Underground Organization or WUO, who later worked with the Black Liberation Army) notes, one group within the WUO had planned an attack "directed at a military ball, [which] would have killed some officers and their dates, thus sinking into a cavalier attitude toward human life and 'collateral damage' all too reminiscent of the US government." See Gilbert, *Love and Struggle* (Oakland: PM Press, 2012), 150. He does not mention it, but there likely would have been other civilian employees working at the event, a fact that underlines the seemingly indiscriminate nature of the targeting in this case.

19 Ann Hansen, "Armed Struggle, Guerilla Warfare, and the Social Movement Influences on 'Direct Action,'" in Best and Nocella, eds., *Igniting a Revolution*, 344.

20 John Clearwater, *"Just Dummies": Cruise Missile Testing in Canada* (Calgary: University of Calgary Press, 2006), 102.

21 The Direct Action Communiqué containing the apology, "Statement Regarding the October 14 Litton Bombing," is reprinted as an appendix to Ann Hansen, *Direct Action: Memoirs of an Urban Guerrilla* (Toronto: Between the Lines, 2001), 477–81.

22 Direct Action Communiqué, 480.

23 Irwin Unger, *The Movement: A History of the American New Left, 1959–1972* (New York: Dodd, Mead and Co., 1975), 180–82.

24 David Gilbert, *Love and Struggle* (Oakland: PM Press, 2012), 162.

25 For historical background on what I here call "sabotage-oriented" environmentalism, see Kim Stallwood, "A Personal Overview of Direct Action in the United Kingdom and the United States," in Steven Best and Anthony Nocella II, eds., *Terrorists or Freedom Fighters? Reflections on the Liberation of Animals* (New York: Lantern Books, 2004), 81–90; and the editors' introduction to Best and Nocella, eds., *Igniting a Revolution*, 8–29.

26 Noel Molland, "A Spark That Ignited a Flame: The Evolution of the Earth Liberation Front," in Best and Nocella, eds., *Igniting a Revolution*, 53.
27 Ibid., 56.
28 Ibid., 54.
29 The communiqué is published in the original Spanish and in English translation on the *Bite Back* website, www.directaction.info.
30 See Will Potter, *Green Is the New Red: An Insider's Account of a Social Movement under Siege* (San Francisco: City Lights, 2011).
31 See John S. Dryzek, *Deliberative Democracy and Beyond: Liberals, Critics, Contestations* (Oxford: Oxford University Press, 2000), chapter 6; Robin Eckersley, *The Green State: Rethinking Sovereignty and Democracy* (Cambridge, MA: MIT Press, 2004); and Michael Saward, "Representation," in Andrew Dobson and Robin Eckersley, eds., *Political Theory and the Ecological Challenge* (Cambridge, MA: Cambridge University Press, 2006), 181–99.
32 See Andrew Dobson, "Democracy and Nature: Speaking and Listening," *Political Studies* 58,4 (October 2010), 752–68; Andrew Dobson, "Democratizing Green Theory: Preconditions and Principles," in B. Doherty and M. de Geus, eds., *Democracy and Green Political Thought: Sustainability, Rights and Citizenship* (London: Routledge, 1996); and Kristian Skagen Ekeli, "Green Constitutionalism: The Constitutional Protection of Future Generations," *Ratio Juris* 20,3 (September 2007), 378–401.
33 John Dryzek, "Green Reason: Communicative Ethics for the Biosphere," *Environmental Ethics* 12 (1990), 195–210.
34 For my own earlier attempt to address these issues, see Stephen D'Arcy, "Deliberative Democracy, Direct Action, and Animal Advocacy," *Journal for Critical Animal Studies* 5,2 (2007), 1–16.
35 See Potter, *Green Is the New Red.*

Seven: The Black Bloc

1 Gerry McNeilly, *Policing the Right to Protest: G20 Systemic Review Report* (Toronto: Office of the Independent Police Review Director, 2012), 138.
2 Timothy Appleby, "Huge Database of Pictures, Video Played Key Role in Tracking G20 Suspects," *Globe and Mail*, March 20, 2013.
3 The Movement Defence Committee, a working group of the Law Union of Ontario, documented several violations of the law by the police and other public officials, including police harassment and illegal detentions and searches; illegal use of preventative arrest and detention; violations of procedural rights; mistreatment, abuse, and neglect of detainees; and mass violations of the Canadian Human Rights Act and the Ontario Human Rights Code. The committee accused the police of "blatant disregard for the law," and condemned the refusal of high-level public officials to hold the police accountable for these actions. See Movement Defence Committee, "Police Violence and State Repression at the Toronto G20: The Facts," in Tom Malleson and David Wachsmuth, eds., *Whose Streets? The Toronto G20 and the Challenges of Summit Protest* (Toronto: Between the Lines, 2011), 87–96.

4 Zig Zag, *Fire and Flames! A Militant Report on Toronto Anti-G20 Resistance* (Zig Zag, July 2010), 23. Zig Zag estimates the size of the bloc as "approximately 100–150 strong, with another 300 or so masked militants not in black." Perhaps counting the group of people not in black, Lesley Wood puts the "black bloc" number at "over 500," in Wood, *Direct Action, Deliberation, and Diffusion: Collective Action after the WTO Protests in Seattle* (Cambridge: Cambridge University Press, 2012), 112. I was present during the breakaway march, where the bloc and others left the main march, and I believe that 150 is an accurate estimate of the number in the black bloc proper.

5 For instance, Graeber, *The Democracy Project*, 13n; Jeff Shantz, *Active Anarchy: Political Practice in Contemporary Movements* (Lanham, MD: Lexington Books, 2011), 50.

6 Zig Zag, *Fire and Flames!*.

7 Dalia al-Sheikh, "Egyptian 'Black Bloc' Is New Force in Protests," *Al-Monitor* [translated from *Al-Hayat*], February 5, 2013.

8 David Graeber, "The New Anarchists," *New Left Review* 13 (January–February 2002), 65.

9 David Van Deusen, "The Emergence of the Black Bloc and the Movement towards Anarchism," in D. Van Deusen and Xavier Massot, eds., *The Black Bloc Papers* (Shawnee Mission, KS: Breaking Glass Press, 2010), 10.

10 CrimethInc. and the Institute for Experimental Freedom, *God Only Knows What Devils We Are: An Apologia for the Black Bloc* (2012), http://zinelibrary.info.

11 CrimethInc., *Recipes for Disaster*, 128.

12 See AK Thompson, *Black Bloc, White Riot: Anti-globalization and the Genealogy of Dissent* (Oakland: AK Press, 2010), 115–16. According to David Graeber, in *The Democracy Project*, 13n, black bloc participants are "usually anarchists."

13 For a detailed history of the Autonomists of Central Europe, notably Germany, see George Katsiaficas, *The Subversion of Politics: European Autonomous Social Movements and the Decolonization of Everyday Life*, updated ed. (Oakland: AK Press, 2006). For a more idiosyncratic but engaging look at the same milieu, see Geronimo, *Fire and Flames: A History of the German Autonomist Movement*, trans. Gabriel Kuhn (Oakland: PM Press, 2012). For a reliable history of Italian Autonomist Marxism, see Steve Wright, *Storming Heaven: Class Composition and Struggle in Italian Autonomist Marxism* (London: Pluto Press, 2002).

14 Sina Rahmani, "Macht Kaputt Was Euch Kaputt Macht: On the History and the Meaning of the Black Block [sic]," *Politics and Culture*, 2009, Issue 4, www.politicsandculture.org.

15 Sturm und drang, "Der Papst ist tot! 25 Jahre Schwarzer Block," *Trend Onlinezeitung*, June 2005, http://trend.infopartisan.net.

16 Georgy Katsiafacas, *The Subversion of Politics: European Autonomous Social Movements and the Decolonization of Everyday Life* (Oakland: AK Press, 2006), 108; cf. Graeber, "The New Anarchists," 66.

17 Zig Zag, *Fire and Flames!*, 22.

18 David Van Deusen and Xavier Massot, eds., *The Black Bloc Papers* (Shawnee Mission, KS: Breaking Glass Press, 2010), 35.

19 Ibid.

20 Francis Dupuis-Déri, "The Black Blocs Ten Years after Seattle," *Journal for the Study of Radicalism* 4,2 (2010), 47.
21 Rebecca Solnit, "Throwing Out the Master's Tools, and Building a Better House" in Carla Blumenkranz, et al., eds., *Occupy! Scenes from Occupied America* (London: Verso, 2011), 148, 151.
22 Chris Hedges, "The Cancer in Occupy," Truthdig, February 6, 2012, www.truthdig.com.
23 CrimethInc., *Recipes for Disaster*, 10–14. All of these points (rage, revulsion against capitalism, and the temporary sense of efficacy) are covered in Sian Sullivan, "'We Are Heartbroken and Furious!': Violence and the (Anti-) Globalization Movement(s)," working paper, University of Warwick, Centre for the Study of Globalisation and Regionalisation, Coventry.
24 Derrick Jensen, quoted in Hedges, "The Cancer in Occupy."
25 CrimethInc., *Recipes for Disaster*, 131.
26 Quoted in Shantz, *Active Anarchy*, 52.
27 Dupuis-Déri, "The Black Blocs Ten Years after Seattle," 56.
28 Evan Mills, "Insurance in a Climate of Change," *Science* 309 (August 12, 2005), 1040.
29 From a different point of view, the pedagogical role of black blocs is also underlined by AK Thompson, in *Black Bloc, White Riot*.
30 Shantz, *Active Anarchy*, 53.
31 CrimethInc., "Breaking News from the Pittsburgh G20 Protests" (2009), www.crimethinc.com.
32 Georgy Katsiafacas, *The Subversion of Politics: European Autonomous Social Movements and the Decolonization of Everyday Life* (Oakland: AK Press, 2006), 124–28.
33 For a detailed account, see chapter 4 of David Graeber, *Direct Action: An Ethnography* (Oakland: AK Press, 2009).
34 See Mark LeVine, "The Revolution, Back in Black," *Al Jazeera Online*, www.aljazeera.com; Zeinab El Guindy, "Meet the Black Bloc: Egypt's Most Talked About Radical Opposition Group," *Ahram Online*, http://english.ahram.org.eg.
35 Zig Zag, *Fire and Flames!*, 19–21.
36 A promising approach for a defender of pedagogical blocs might be found in Alan Sears's Brechtian conception of popular education, as developed in his book *Retooling the Mind Factory* (Toronto: Garamond, 2003), 246–58.

Eight: Rioting

1 King, "I Have a Dream," 103.
2 Even the ultimate Establishment spokesperson, US president Obama, conceded that the Stonewall Riot (although he carefully avoided using the word) was a force for democratization. See the *New York Times* editorial "Beyond Selma-to-Stonewall," January 27, 2013.
3 Andrew Kopkind, "After Stonewall," *The Thirty Years War: Dispatches and Diversions of a Radical Journalist, 1965–1994* (London: Verso, 1996), 513.
4 For a brief yet detail-rich account of the events, see Martin Duberman, "The Night They Raided Stonewall," *Grand Street* 11 (1993), 121–47. For the wider context and impact, see Duberman's important book *Stonewall* (New York: Plume, 1994).

5 See William P. Jones, *The March on Washington: Jobs, Freedom and the Forgotten History of Civil Rights* (New York: W.W. Norton & Co., 2013).

6 See Jeremy Varon, *Bringing the War Home: The Weather Underground, the Red Army Faction, and Revolutionary Violence in the Sixties and Seventies* (Berkeley: University of California Press, 2004), 74–112. Note that I assume here that the Days of Rage confrontation was not a riot, or at least not a riot of the usual sort, because it was planned and co-ordinated by an organized group. Arguably, it is much closer to the black bloc phenomenon than it is to the LA Riots or Stonewall.

7 Thomas Ellwood, *A Discourse Concerning Riots* (London: Thomas Howkins, 1683), 11. I have slightly altered the spelling of a few words, and removed some italics, in keeping with the conventions of modern English.

8 In Canada's Criminal Code, "an unlawful assembly is an assembly of three or more persons who, with intent to carry out any common purpose, assemble in such a manner or so conduct themselves when they are assembled as to cause persons in the neighbourhood of the assembly to fear, on reasonable grounds, that they (a) will disturb the peace tumultuously; or (b) will by that assembly and without reasonable cause provoke other persons to disturb the peace tumultuously" (R.S., c. C-34, s. 64). Further, "a riot is an unlawful assembly that has begun to disturb the peace tumultuously" (R.S., c. C-34, s. 65). See http://laws-lois.justice.gc.ca.

9 In US law, "the term 'riot' means a public disturbance involving an act or acts of violence by one or more persons part of an assemblage of three or more persons, which act or acts shall constitute a clear and present danger of, or shall result in, damage or injury to the property of any other person or to the person of any other individual," or credible threats thereof. See www.law.cornell.edu.

10 Public Order Act 1986 (UK). See www.legislation.gov.uk.

11 See George Rudé, *The Crowd in History: A Study of Popular Disturbances in France and England, 1730–1848*, rev. ed. (London: Lawrence and Wishart, 1981); E.P. Thompson, *The Making of the English Working Class* (New York: Vintage, 1966); E.J. Hobsbawm and George Rudé, *Captain Swing* (London: Lawrence & Wishart, 1968).

12 See Jemma Purdey, *Anti-Chinese Violence in Indonesia, 1996–1999* (Singapore: Singapore University Press, 2006), 122–24.

13 There are indications that some of these attacks were "state-sponsored," namely, by the Indonesian military. But I cannot delve into the details here. See ibid, 147–56.

14 Dave Zirin, "The Fans Who Fan the Flames: Egypt's Ultras at the Crossroads," *The Nation*, July 4, 2013. See also Gabriel Kuhn, *Soccer vs. the State: Tackling Football and Radical Politics* (Oakland: PM Press, 2011). For an alarming look at the Italian far-right version of politicized soccer fan culture, see Alberto Testa and Gary Armstrong, *Football, Fascism and Fandom: The Ultras of Italian Football* (London: A&C Black, 2010).

15 For some contemporary research on anti-Semitic pogroms in Eastern Europe, into the early twentieth century, see Jonathan Dekel-Chen, David Gaunt, Natan Meir, and Israel Bartal, *Anti-Jewish Violence: Rethinking the Pogrom in East European History* (Bloomington: Indiana University Press, 2010).

16 Gerald Horne, *Fire This Time: The Watts Uprising and the 1960s* (NY: Da Capo Press, 1997), 355–56.

17 Ibid., 356.

18 Brenda Stevenson, *The Contested Murder of Latasha Harlins: Justice, Gender, and the Origins of the LA Riots* (Oxford: Oxford University Press, 2013).

19 For two helpful recent articles reviewing and reflecting on the uprising, see Nigel Gibson, "20 Years After the L.A. Riots, Revisiting the Rationality of Revolt," Truthout, May 12, 2012, http://truth-out.org; and Lewis Gordon, "Of Illicit Appearance: The L.A. Riots/Rebellion as a Portent of Things to Come," Truthout, May 12, 2012, http://truth-out.org. For a detailed yet concise review of the events and their context, see chapter 7 of Janet L. Abu-Lughod, *Race, Space, and Riots in Chicago, New York, and Los Angeles* (Oxford: Oxford University Press, 2007); see also Kamran Afary, *Performance and Activism: Grassroots Discourse after the Los Angeles Rebellion of 1992* (New York: Lexington Books, 2009), for a discussion of some of the impacts on Los Angeles neighbourhoods and the response of community organizations to the rebellion's aftermath.

20 Martin Luther King, Jr., "Conscience for Change," 202.

21 Ibid.

22 Zygmunt Bauman, "The London Riots – On Consumerism Coming Home to Roost," *Social Europe Journal*, August 9, 2011, www.social-europe.eu.

23 Slavoj Žižek, "Shoplifters of the World Unite," *London Review of Books*, online only article, August 19, 2011, www.lrb.co.uk.

24 See Sarah Anne Hughes, "BBC Apologizes to Darcus Howe for 'Poorly Phrased Question,'" *Washington Post* online, August 11, 2011, www.washingtonpost.com.

25 CBC News, "A Tale of Two Riots: Comparing the 1994 and 2011 Stanley Cup Riots in Vancouver," www.cbc.ca.

26 Bethany Lindsay, "From Bad to Brutal: Timeline of a Riot," CTV News website, published July 16, 2011; updated May 19, 2012, http://bc.ctvnews.ca.

27 See Dave Zirin, "Understanding Vancouver's 'Hockey Riot,'" a blog entry posted at the website of *The Nation* a few days after the riot, www.thenation.com.

28 Alan Steinweis, *Kristallnacht* (Cambridge, MA: Harvard University Press, 2009), 61.

29 Oklahoma Commission to Study the Tulsa Race Riot of 1921, *Tulsa Race Riot: A Report*, February 28, 2001, www.okhistory.org.

30 "A Story from the LA Riots," *Natural Newark*, April 28, 2012, www.naturalnewark.com.

31 This objection is made by Martin Luther King, Jr., in "Where Do We Go from Here?" 1967, in Washington, ed., *I Have a Dream*, 174–75.

32 Albert O. Hirschman, *Exit, Voice, and Loyalty: Responses to Decline in Organizations, Firms, and States* (Cambridge: Harvard University Press, 1970).

33 Habermas, *Legitimation Crisis*, 37.

34 David J. Olson, "Riot Commissions and Political Change," in Philip Meranto, ed., *The Kerner Report Revisited* (Urbana, IL: Institute of Government and Public Affairs, 1970), 169.

35 Lindsey Lupo, *Flak-Catchers: One Hundred Years of Riot Commission Politics in America* (Lanham, MD: Lexington Books, 2011), 237.

Nine: Armed Struggle

1 Angelique Chrisafis, "Rural Idyll or Terrorist Hub? The Village That Police Say Is a Threat to the State," *The Guardian*, January 3, 2009.

2 Invisible Committee. *The Coming Insurrection* (Los Angeles: Semiotext(e), 2009), 128–29.

3 There is room for some debate about exactly what strategy the Invisible Committee proposes, due mainly to the ambiguity of their writing. But they seem consciously to invoke the imagery of urban guerrilla militancy, calling not only for armed insurrection in general terms, but more specifically for "a moving multiplicity that can strike a number of places at once and that tries to always keep the initiative" (*The Coming Insurrection*, 116).

4 For my purposes, "armed struggle" refers to intentionally using armed force to kill or injure people. Some groups, like Direct Action in Canada, injured people accidentally, but did not target them intentionally, and I therefore do not treat them as armed struggle groups in this chapter. For the same reason, I exclude the Black Panther Party and the Deacons for Defense, which advocated armed self-defence, but not the tactical use of armed attacks as part of a political or military strategy. In this sense, armed struggle should not be taken literally, to mean "struggling while armed," but rather as a technical term referring to the tactical use of armed force to threaten or kill people.

5 Max Horkheimer and Theodor Adorno, *The Dialectic of Enlightenment: Philosophical Fragments* (Stanford: Stanford University Press, 2002); Herbert Marcuse, *One-Dimensional Man: Studies in the Ideology of Advanced Industrial Society* (Boston: Beacon Press, 1964); Paul Goodman, *Growing Up Absurd: Problems of Youth in the Organized System* (New York: Vintage, 1960); Tom Hayden, *The Port Huron Statement* (New York: Thunder's Mouth Press, 2005; originally published by Students for a Democratic Society, 1962); Guy Debord, *The Society of the Spectacle* (New York: Zone Books, 1995).

6 This oft-cited aphorism first appears in the *Second Declaration of Havana* (Detroit: Radical Education Project, 1971), 17. The Declaration was issued by the Cuban government in 1962, and is often attributed to Fidel Castro.

7 Andrew Fiala, *Practical Pacifism* (New York: Algora Publishing, 2004), 13.

8 David Blitz, "Russell, Einstein and the Philosophy of Non-absolute Pacifism," *Russell: The Journal of Bertrand Russell Studies* 20 (Winter 2000–01), 101–28.

9 Fiala, *Practical Pacifism*, 22.

10 The idea that defence against aggression is the only just grounds for the use of force is associated with traditional just war theory. Although just war theory originated in Catholic religious thought in the Middle Ages, it has in recent years been used by a number of thinkers to explore the ethics of armed revolution. See Michael Walzer, *Just and Unjust Wars: A Moral Argument with Historical Illustrations* (New York: Basic Books, 1977), notably chapter 11, on guerrilla warfare; Norman Geras, "Our Morals: The Ethics of Revolution," *Socialist Register* 25 (1989), 185–211; Ann E. Cudd, *Analyzing Oppression* (Oxford: Oxford University Press, 2006).

11 For two important studies of armed self-defence in the context of the US Civil Rights movement, see Akinyele Omowale Umoja, *We Will Shoot Back: Armed Resistance in the*

Mississippi Freedom Movement (New York: NYU Press, 2013); and Lance Hill, *The Deacons of Defense: Armed Resistance and the Civil Rights Movement* (Chapel Hill: University of North Carolina Press, 2006).

12 Marx, "The Civil War in France."

13 Donny Gluckstein, "Militia and Workers' State: Paris 1871," in Mike Gonzalez and Houman Barekat, eds., *Arms and the People: Popular Movements and the Military from the Paris Commune to the Arab Spring* (London: Pluto Press, 2013), 105–22.

14 Donny Gluckstein, *The Paris Commune: A Revolution in Democracy* (London: Bookmarks Publications, 2006), 177.

15 Ward Churchill, *Pacifism as Pathology: Reflections on the Role of Armed Struggle in North America* (Edinburgh: AK Press, c2007), 50.

16 Karl Marx and Friedrich Engels, *The Communist Manifesto* (Peterborough, ON: Broadview, 2004; originally 1848), 94.

17 The term "systemic violence" seems to be a variant of the earlier concept of "structural violence," introduced by Johan Galtung, "Violence, Peace, and Peace Research," *Journal of Peace Research* 6,3 (1969), 167–91.

18 Slavoj Žižek, *Violence* (London: Profile Books, 2009), 1.

19 Woody Guthrie, "Pretty Boy Floyd," 1958.

20 International Commission on Intervention and State Sovereignty (ICISS), *The Responsibility to Protect* (Ottawa: International Development Research Centre, 2001), 17.

21 Ibid., 32.

22 Fernando Téson, "Ending Tyranny in Iraq," *Ethics and International Affairs* (2005).

23 Peter Singer, *One World: The Ethics of Globalization* (London: Yale University Press, 2002), 125.

24 For a popular recounting of the history of the Dublin Lockout, see chapter 11 of Peter Berresford Ellis, *A History of the Irish Working Class* (London: Pluto, 1996).

25 ITGWU president Jim Larkin, quoted in Sean O'Casey, *The Story of the Irish Citizen Army* (Honolulu, Hawaii: University Press of the Pacific, 2003; originally published in 1919 under the name P.O. Cathasaigh), 4–5.

26 Ibid., 9.

27 Ibid., 14.

28 John O'Connor, "The Zapatistas Today: An Interview with John Ross," *Against the Current* 22,4 (September/October 2007), 16–17.

29 Chris Tilly and Marie Kennedy, "Counter-campaigns and Autonomous Communities: The Zapatistas' New Fight," *Against the Current* 21,3 (July/August 2006), 21–25.

30 Curtis J. Austin, *Up against the Wall: Violence in the Making and Unmaking of the Black Panther Party* (Fayetteville: University of Arkansas Press, 2008); Nelson Blackstock, *Cointelpro: The FBI's Secret War on Political Freedom* (New York: Pathfinder Press, 1988).

31 Akinyele Omowale Umoja, "Repression Breeds Resistance: The Black Liberation Army and the Radical Legacy of the Black Panther Party," *New Political Science* 21,2 (1999), 139.

32 Coordinating Committee, Black Liberation Army, *Message to the Black Movement: A Political Statement from the Black Underground* (BLA: 1976), 3–4.

33 Red Army Faction, "Build the Red Army!," June 5, 1970, in J. Smith and André Moncourt, eds., *The Red Army Faction: A Documentary History, Volume 1: Projectiles for the People* (Montreal: Kersplebedeb Publishing and Distribution, 2009), 79–82.

34 Red Army Faction, "The Urban Guerrilla Concept," April 1971, in ibid., 98.

35 See "Armed Struggle in West Germany: A Chronology," in J. Smith and Andre Moncourt, *The Red Army Faction: A Documentary History, Vol. 2: Dancing with Imperialism* (Montreal: Kersplebedeb, 2013), 368.

36 A detailed typology of different forms of armed struggle is offered in T. Derbent, *Categories of Revolutionary Military Policy* (Montreal: Kersplebedeb, 2006), 17–24.

37 For the classic articulation of the case for militarist vanguardism, i.e., the idea that the left should be led by armed guerrilla "nucleus" formations, see Régis Debray, *Revolution in the Revolution?* (New York: Grove Press, 1967). Debray writes: "Under certain conditions, the political and the military are not separate, but form one organic whole, consisting of the people's army, whose nucleus is the guerrilla army. The vanguard party can exist in the form of the guerrilla *foco* itself. The guerrilla force is the party in embryo" (106). Note, however, that he has the Cuban revolution in mind, not even-more-tiny guerrilla bands in places like Germany or France.

38 The motif of "clean hands" and "dirty hands," and the depiction of noncombatant immunity as a petit bourgeois or middle-class notion, has its roots in Jean-Paul Sartre's 1948 play *Dirty Hands*, in which socialists grapple with the ethics of assassination, among other themes. One character utters these famous lines: "How you cling to your purity, young man! How afraid you are to soil your hands! All right, stay pure! What good will it do? Purity is an idea for a yogi or a monk. You intellectuals and bourgeois anarchists use it as a pretext for doing nothing. To do nothing, to remain motionless, arms at your sides, wearing kid gloves. Well, I have dirty hands. Right in to the elbows. You don't love men, Hugo. You love only principles." See Sartre, *No Exit and Three Other Plays* (New York: Vintage, 1989), 218. Out of context, this may seem like a point about armed struggle or noncombatant immunity, but in context it is offered as a rationale for supporting alliances with sections of the ruling class. What links these two ideas is the elevation of pragmatic power politics above considerations of political principle and the dubious stigmatization of any principled stance as alien to the workers' movement.

39 Certainly, the left has had experience of militancy that installed new elites in power, little or no better than those they replaced. The conventional stratagem of depicting every such case as a unique act of betrayal by treacherous individuals is no longer convincing. For a critique of the betrayal theory of why some left revolts end in authoritarian rule by "Party" elites, see John Holloway, *Change the World without Taking Power*, 2nd ed. (London: Pluto Press, 2005), 12–13.

40 I draw out the strategic implications of the left's marginalization for anticapitalist activism in Stephen D'Arcy, "Strategy, Meta-strategy, and Anti-capitalist Activism," *Socialist Studies* 5,2 (2009), 64–89.

41 For an account of how the left can move in the direction suggested here, see Stephen

D'Arcy, "A Civil Society Strategy for Revitalizing the Left," *The Bullet* 543 (September 11, 2011), www.socialistproject.ca.

42 For an unusually friendly exchange from a few years ago, see the article by Marxists Todd Gordon and Jerome Klassen, "Anarchism, Marxism, and Renewing Socialism from Below," and the "Comments" offered in response by anarchist Wayne Price, originally published on the New Socialist website (newsocialist.org), and now available here: http://nefac.net. For an interpretation of anarchism that underlines its proximity to key aspects of early Marxism, see Lucien van der Walt and Michael Schmidt, *Black Flame: The Revolutionary Class Politics of Anarchism and Syndicalism* (Oakland: AK Press, 2009).

43 Karl Marx, "Critique of the Gotha Programme," 1875, www.marxists.org.

44 For a more detailed and nuanced discussion of the political relationship between Bakunin and Marx than I can provide here, see Tom Keefer, "Marxism, Anarchism, and the Genealogy of 'Socialism from Below,'" *Upping the Anti: A Journal of Theory and Action* 2 (2005), 58–81.

45 As Marx and Engels put the point in an 1879 letter: "When the International was formed we expressly formulated the battle-cry: the emancipation of the working class must be achieved by the working class itself. We cannot therefore cooperate with people who say that the workers are too uneducated to emancipate themselves and must first be freed from above by philanthropic bourgeois or petty bourgeois" (Marx and Engels, Circular Letter to Bebel, et al., September 1879), www.marxists.org.

Index